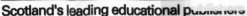

Leckie×Leckie

Scotland's leading educational publishers

CfE Higher
MODERN STUDIES
SUCCESS GUIDE

CfE Higher MODERN STUDIES SUCCESS GUIDE

© 2016 Leckie & Leckie Ltd
Cover © ink-tank and associates

001/15122015

10 9 8 7 6 5 4 3 2 1

ISBN 9780007554454

Published by
Leckie & Leckie Ltd
An imprint of HarperCollins*Publishers*
Westerhill Road, Bishopbriggs, Glasgow, G64 2QT
T: 0844 576 8126   F: 0844 576 8131
leckieandleckie@harpercollins.co.uk
www.leckieandleckie.co.uk

Commissioning editor: Katherine Wilkinson
Project manager: Keren McGill

Special thanks to
Jill Laidlaw (proofread)
Louise Robb (proofread and copy edit)
QBS (layout and illustrations)

Printed in Italy by Grafica Veneta S.P.A.

A CIP Catalogue record for this book is available from the British Library.

Acknowledgements

We would like to thank the following for permission to reproduce their material:

P23a © chrisdorney / Shutterstock.com; P26a © Atlaspix / Shutterstock.com; P26b © 360b / Shutterstock.com; P26c © UniversalImagesGroup / Contributor; P26d © Oli Scarff / Staff; P26e ©Cornfield / Shutterstock.com; P27 © WPA Pool / Pool / Getty Images; P29 © Frederic Legrand - COMEO / Shutterstock.com; P30 © Oli Scarff / Staff / Getty Images; P33 © Jeff Morgan 08 / Alamy Stock Photo; P35 © Anadolu Agency / Contributor / Getty Images; P37 © WPA Pool / Pool / Getty Images; P38 © Jeremy Sutton-Hibbert / Contributor / Getty Images; P39 © Chris Watt / Stringer / Getty Images; P40 © Jeff J Mitchell / Staff / Getty Images; P42 ©WPA Pool / Pool . Getty Images; P45 © Jeff J Mitchell / Staff / Getty Images; P46 © Handout / Handout / Getty Images; P47 © Jeff J Mitchell / Staff / Getty Images; P49 © Ian MacNicol / Stringer / Getty Images; P65 © Matt Cardy / Stringer / Getty Images; P66 © LEON NEAL / Staff / Getty Images; P67 © Dave Thompson / Stringer / Getty Images; P69 © Jeff J Mitchell / Staff / Getty Images; P71 © News UK, P72 © News UK; P74 © Jeremy Sutton-Hibbert / Contributor / Getty Images; P81 © Jeff J Mitchell / Staff / Getty Images; P84 © Bloomberg / Contributor / Getty Images; P86 © SergeBertasiusPhotography / Shutterstock. co____ ___ © OLI SCARFF / Stringer / Getty Images; P95 © O____ __ Staff / Getty Images; P96 © Stuart C. Wilson ___ / Getty Images; P100a Taken by Mnbf9rca ____nglish Wikipedia and licensed under the Creative ___ons Attribution-Share Alike 2.5 Generic license; ___ chrisdorney / Shutterstock.com; P106 © Alex ___re / Contributor; P111 © Mary Evans Picture Library / Alamy Stock Photo; P113 © Geoffrey Robinson / Alamy Stock Photo ;P115 © 1000 Words / Shutterstock.com; P117 © John Phillips / Contributor / Getty Images; P118 © Iain McGillivray / Shutterstock.com; P120 © WENN Ltd / Alamy Stock Photo; P121 © © Steven May / Alamy Stock Photo; P122 © Elena Rostunova / Shutterstock.com; P125 © Stephen Barnes/Law and Order / Alamy Stock Photo; P133 © Chip Somodevilla / Staff / Getty Images; P135 © MANDEL NGAN / Staff / Getty Images; P137 © NetPhotos / Alamy Stock Photo; P140 © FREDERIC J. BROWN / Staff / Getty Images; P145 © Shutterstock. com; P146 © Ethan Miller / Staff / Getty Images; P151 © weerapong pumpradit / Shutterstock.com; P157a © PIUS UTOMI EKPEI / Stringer / Getty Images; P158 © Boston Globe / Contributor / Getty Images; P159 © conejota / Shutterstock.com; P161 © MAHMUD HAMS / Staff / Getty Images; P163 © Anadolu Agency / Contributor / Getty Images; P164 © Hindustan Times / Contributor / Getty Images; P167 © Matt Cardy / Stringer / Getty Images; P172 © Anadolu Agency / Contributor / Getty Images; P173 © MICHAEL URBAN / Staff / Getty Images

All other images from Shutterstock.com

Questions taken from SQA past and specimen papers reproduced with permission, copyright © Scottish Qualifications Authority.

Contents

The course

Rationale

Studying Modern Studies at Higher will build on the knowledge and skills that you developed within Modern Studies at National 5 or across other areas of the curriculum. The course aims to encourage you to think critically about the society we live in, widening your knowledge of political, social and international issues, while encouraging you to consider the values and beliefs of others. As a result, the course will prepare you for your place in society as a responsible citizen who is able to make an effective contribution both at home and beyond.

You will engage in investigative and critical thinking activities, allowing you to work collaboratively with peers as well as developing your skills as an independent learner. Furthermore you will build on your capacity to evaluate and analyse a wide range of sources, allowing you to make informed decisions, come to valid conclusions, and hone your ability to identify where sources have been selective in the use of facts. These transferable skills will support you as you move on to Further or Higher Education or the world of work.

Think about your place in the world

Course outline

The Higher course consists of three units. Within these course units there is considerable choice with regard to the topics studied. This Success Guide offers support for the units shown in the table below.

Unit title	Topics covered in the Success Guide
Political issues	Democracy in Scotland and the United Kingdom
Social issues	• Social inequality in the United Kingdom • Crime and the law in the United Kingdom
International issues	• World power – the USA • World issue – terrorism

Assessment

In order to pass Higher Modern Studies you must complete the **three** areas of assessment.

Unit Assessment → Assignment → Course Assessment The Exam

Unit assessment

Throughout the year, unit assessments will be carried out to allow your teacher to gather 'evidence' and assess your 'basic competency' in the course. This will ensure that you are meeting the required standard for Higher Modern Studies. The unit assessments will assess both knowledge and skills, and evidence may be gathered in a number of ways including presentations, information posters, participation in group tasks, responses to questions, or extended writing tasks. There are no restrictions on the resources that you may access during the unit assessments and there are no time restrictions for the unit assessments.

The Assignment

The Assignment is the added value (AVU) element of the course. You may remember this from National 5 Modern Studies or another area of the curriculum. The Assignment has two main elements:

1. Research

2. Production of evidence

TOP TIP

Choose an issue that has clear arguments to support or oppose it.

You will choose an area of study that allows you to analyse a complex contemporary issue and apply decision making skills. You will research the issue, analysing and evaluating sources of evidence.

The Assignment is worth 30 marks and is part of the course assessment. There is more information on the Assignment on pages 21–5.

The Exam

The Exam will consist of **one** question paper. It will assess your skills and breadth of knowledge and understanding across the three units of the course. The question paper will also assess your ability to.

• Detect and explain the degree of objectivity using a range of sources of information.

• Draw and support complex conclusions using a range of sources of information.

• Give detailed explanations and analysis of complex issues.

The question paper is worth 60 marks (44 marks for knowledge and understanding (KU) and 16 for skills) and will be divided into three sections in line with the three units covered – (i) Democracy in Scotland and the UK, (ii) Social issues in the UK and (iii) International issues. Each section of the paper is worth 20 marks. The time allocated for the question paper is 2 hours and 15 minutes.

Knowledge and understanding

In both the unit and course assessments at Higher you will be expected to answer knowledge and understanding (KU) questions.

Unit assessments

Each unit has specific knowledge outcomes that you must achieve. These will be assessed internally by your teacher on a pass/fail basis. The evidence for this assessment task can be generated in a variety of forms including, for example, presentations, information posters, participation in group tasks, responses to questions, or extended writing. There are no restrictions on the resources you may have access to during this unit assessment and there are no time restrictions for completing the task.

Democracy in Scotland and the United Kingdom

You will be asked to draw on factual and theoretical knowledge and understanding of democracy in the Scottish and United Kingdom political systems by:

1. Giving detailed descriptions and detailed explanations of a complex political issue, which draw on a factual and theoretical knowledge and understanding of democracy in Scotland/the United Kingdom.

2. Analysing a complex political issue in Scotland/the United Kingdom.

Social issues in the United Kingdom

You will be asked to draw on factual and theoretical knowledge and understanding of social issues in the United Kingdom, focusing on either social inequality **or** crime and the law by:

1. Giving detailed descriptions and detailed explanations that draw on a factual and theoretical knowledge and understanding of a complex social issue in the United Kingdom.

2. Analysing a complex social issue in the United Kingdom.

International issues

You will be asked to draw on factual and theoretical knowledge and understanding of international issues, focusing on either a major world power **or** a significant world issue by:

1. Giving detailed descriptions and detailed explanations that draw on a factual and theoretical knowledge and understanding of a complex international issue.

2. Analysing a complex international issue.

Course assessment – the Exam

The final Exam is allocated 2 hours and 15 minutes and is worth a total of 60 marks. It is split into three sections, each worth 20 marks. Each section will ask either a knowledge question (12 marks) **and** a skills question (8 marks) totalling 20 marks, or simply a 20-mark knowledge question. This will change from year to year.

There are four types of KU question in the final Exam, worth between 12 and 20 marks. They involve four key command words/phrases, which are each allocated a specific number of marks.

These questions can appear in any section of the paper.

Key command word/phrase	Number of marks
Analyse	12
Evaluate	12
To what extent	20
Discuss	20

The front page of the question paper looks similar to the information below. In each section you have studied there will be a choice of two questions for you to answer, as shown on the next page.

TOP TIP

Ensure that you are fully aware of which **part** within each **section** you should answer questions on. For example, in the paper shown on the next page, everyone will answer the knowledge questions in Section 1 – **either** 1(a) **or** 1(b). However you must select Part A **or** B in both sections 2 and 3, i.e. if you have studied 'Crime and the law in the United Kingdom', answer 3(c) **or** 3(d) and if you have studied a World Power, such as South Africa or China perhaps, answer 5(a) **or** 5(b).

The course and the assessment

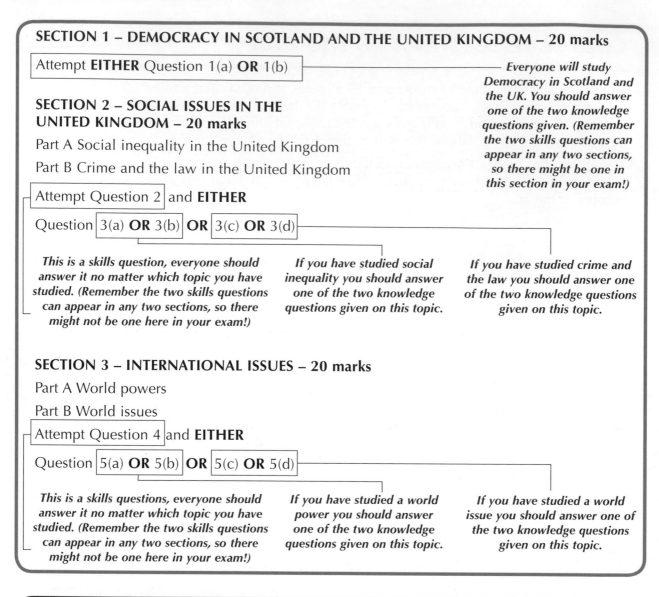

SECTION 1 – DEMOCRACY IN SCOTLAND AND THE UNITED KINGDOM – 20 marks

Attempt **EITHER** Question 1(a) **OR** 1(b) ———— *Everyone will study Democracy in Scotland and the UK. You should answer one of the two knowledge questions given. (Remember the two skills questions can appear in any two sections, so there might be one in this section in your exam!)*

SECTION 2 – SOCIAL ISSUES IN THE UNITED KINGDOM – 20 marks

Part A Social inequality in the United Kingdom

Part B Crime and the law in the United Kingdom

Attempt Question 2 and **EITHER**

Question 3(a) **OR** 3(b) **OR** 3(c) **OR** 3(d)

This is a skills question, everyone should answer it no matter which topic you have studied. (Remember the two skills questions can appear in any two sections, so there might not be one here in your exam!)

If you have studied social inequality you should answer one of the two knowledge questions given on this topic.

If you have studied crime and the law you should answer one of the two knowledge questions given on this topic.

SECTION 3 – INTERNATIONAL ISSUES – 20 marks

Part A World powers

Part B World issues

Attempt Question 4 and **EITHER**

Question 5(a) **OR** 5(b) **OR** 5(c) **OR** 5(d)

This is a skills questions, everyone should answer it no matter which topic you have studied. (Remember the two skills questions can appear in any two sections, so there might not be one here in your exam!)

If you have studied a world power you should answer one of the two knowledge questions given on this topic.

If you have studied a world issue you should answer one of the two knowledge questions given on this topic.

What is required for 12 and 20 marks?

12-mark questions

In the 12-mark questions you can be awarded up to a maximum of 8 marks for showing your knowledge and understanding of the issue. Try to remember to use the SEE system – make a **s**tatement, give an **e**xplanation of that point and support it with relevant **e**xemplification. The remaining 4 marks are awarded for analysis **or** evaluation of the issue.

So for 12 marks you could achieve 8 by demonstrating **at least two** relevant aspects of knowledge, fully explained, which relate closely to the key aspects of the question **supported by** extended, relevant, accurate and up-to-date examples. You could gain the other 4 marks by giving **at least one** insightful, extended, accurate and justified analytical or evaluative comment, which relates closely to the key aspects of the question and is supported by evidence.

- Knowledge – 8
- Analysis/Evaluation – 4

20-mark questions

- For 20 marks, just as for 12-mark questions, you again will be awarded up to a maximum of 8 marks for KU. The remaining marks are awarded for analysis, evaluation/conclusions **and** structure. You could gain up to 6 marks for demonstrating **at least two** developed, relevant and accurate analytical comments that are justified **and** exemplified. These should relate closely to the question and may be linked. A further 4 marks can be awarded for balanced, insightful conclusions that are justified and directly address the central aspects of the question, considering a range of viewpoints. The final 2 marks are awarded for a structure that identifies the issue and presents a clear and consistent line of argument.
- Knowledge – 8
- Analysis – 6
- Conclusion(s)/Evaluative comments – 4
- Structure – 2

If you make more analytical/evaluative points than are required to gain the maximum allocation of marks, these can be credited as knowledge and understanding marks.

'Analyse' questions

You will be asked to identify parts of an issue, the relationship between these parts and their relationships with the whole. You may also be able to draw out and relate implications to certain issues.

For all of the below sample questions with possible responses, all text in blue is a relevant point with an analytical comment and all text in red is a further relevant point giving extended analytical comment.

Analyse the inequalities faced by certain groups in society.	**12 marks**

Women suffer income inequality. This is evidenced by the Gender Pay Gap. The BBC reported recently that women on average earn 9.4% less than men. This is often attributed to the fact that women take career breaks to have a family and lose valuable experience in the workplace. However the BBC report also highlighted that the gender pay gap had fallen, with women in the age range of 22–40 earning more than men for the first time. It is further argued that new regulations regarding shared maternity leave should help to bridge the gap in earnings.

The above answer would be worthy of 3/4 marks given that the candidate has made two relevant points with extended analytical comment.

Here are some further 'analyse' questions to consider:

- Analyse government policies to tackle inequalities that affect a group in society.
- Analyse the view that poverty is the most important factor that affects health.
- Analyse government policies to tackle crime.
- Analyse the social explanations of crime.

'Evaluate' questions

You will be asked to make a judgement based on criteria; to determine the value of something.

Evaluate the effectiveness of prison in tackling crime.	**12 marks**

Prison is effective in that it removes the offender from environments where they have offended, giving them the opportunity to reflect on their actions, potentially access education or treatment programmes, in turn offering them an opening to change once released. However prisoners serving short-term sentences may not be able to access such programmes due to lack of opportunities in prison and so they may find themselves in identical situations when released. In Scotland reoffending rates vary, however in some areas such as Dundee, which has the highest imprisonment rate in Scotland, more than one in three criminals sentenced in the city pick up another conviction within 12 months. This would suggest that short-term prison sentences may have a limited impact on tackling crime.

This would be worthy of 3/4 marks given that the candidate has made two relevant points with extended analytical/evaluative comment.

Here are some further 'evaluate' questions to consider:

*   Evaluate the importance of lack of success in education as a cause of social inequality.
*   Evaluate the effectiveness of the benefits system in tackling social inequality.
*   Evaluate the importance of lack of success in education as a cause of crime.

'To what extent' questions

You will be asked to analyse the issue in the question and come to a conclusion or conclusions that involve evaluative judgement(s) with regard to how accurate the view is. This should be supported with a detailed justification.

To what extent do Members of the Scottish Parliament (MSPs) influence decision making in the Scottish Government?	**20 marks**

Members of the Scottish Parliament (MSPs) are able to influence decision making as a result of the electoral system used. Using the Additional Member System generally produces a coalition or minority government, which gives ordinary members greater influence. Between 2003 and 2007 the SNP faced a number of challenges from MSPs in their attempts to influence decision making. As a result of having a minority of MSPs in the parliament, the SNP government were often defeated in their attempts to pass legislation given that they often relied on MSPs from other parties to support their bills. This was evident in relation to areas such as Council Tax, Edinburgh Trams and Minimum Pricing on Alcohol. However the election in 2011 produced the uncommon result of a majority government, with the SNP securing 69 of the 129 seats. As a result they have been able to pass legislation that otherwise may have faced challenges. In May 2012 the SNP were eventually able to pass legislation on Minimum Pricing with 86 votes to one, with 32 abstentions, given that Labour would not support the bill. Even with the added support of some of the other parties the SNP could have passed this legislation on its own.

This would be worthy of 5/6 marks given that the candidate has made two developed, relevant and accurate analytical comments that are justified and exemplified. They also relate closely to the question and are linked.

Here are some further 'to what extent' questions to consider:

- To what extent is the media the most important factor affecting voter behaviour?
- To what extent have the government been successful in reducing gender and/or race inequalities in the UK?
- To what extent have government policies reduced poverty in the UK?

'Discuss' questions

In these questions you will communicate ideas and information on the issue in the statement. You will be credited for analysing and evaluating different views of the statement/viewpoint. You should also make a judgement about the accuracy of the statement.

> The political system provides an effective check on the government.
> Discuss with reference to a world power you have studied.   **20 marks**

World power – USA

Within the USA, Congress acts as an effective check on the government in line with constitutional arrangements. However the President and in turn the government has significant powers that are often difficult for Congress to restrict. The President has the power to veto any bill that Congress has passed, simply returning it unsigned with recommendations as to how it could be amended or improved. President Obama has only used his veto three times so far (as of February 2015), whereas George W. Bush used it on 12 occasions during his two terms, with his final veto aiming to restrict the Medicare Improvements for Patients and Providers Act. However Congress is able to override any veto of a bill imposed by the President. In order for the veto to be overridden Congress needs a two-thirds majority in both the Senate and the House of Representatives to vote against it. This appears to be a challenge to Congress as a large number of attempts to override a veto fail. However George W. Bush's final veto was overridden by Congress with both houses passing the number of votes required. It is therefore accurate to state that on certain occasions the political system can be a significant check on the government.

This would be worthy of 5/6 marks given that the candidate has made two developed, relevant and accurate analytical comments that are justified and exemplified. They also relate closely to the question and are linked.

Here are some further 'discuss' questions to consider:

- Health and welfare provision should be the responsibility of the government. Discuss.
- Poverty is the most important factor that affects health. Discuss.
- The additional powers the Scottish Parliament has been given will allow it to better deliver 'Scottish solutions to Scottish problems'. Discuss.
- Government responses have been effective in improving socio-economic issues. Discuss with reference to the world power you have studied.

TOP TIP

You will find the SQA support document to identify past papers that could be used or amended as part of your revision prior to the Exam here: www.sqa.org.uk/files_ccc/ ModernStudiesSQPHPPGuidance.pdf

Drawing and supporting conclusions

You should be able to draw and support complex conclusions using a range of sources of information. In the final Exam, this question can occur in **any** section and will be worth 8 marks overall.

The question will have between two and four sources – conclusions must be drawn from these sources. After the sources you will be able to gain further support from the bullet points acting as a prompt to show you what you should draw a conclusion about.

Steps to success

1. Identify what you are being asked to draw a conclusion on – use the bullet points as a prompt.

2. Identify which sources link to each of the bullet points, highlighting the key information from the sources that you will be able to use to support your conclusions.

3. Remember to use **all** the sources – a maximum of 6 marks will be awarded in the Exam if all sources are not used.

4. Write your answer – remember the key thing is you **must synthesise your sources** – this means comparing the information within and between sources. Up to 3 marks will be awarded for **one** conclusion depending on the appropriate use and synthesis of evidence, in total giving you the opportunity to gain 6 marks. The final 2 marks available are given for an overall, summative conclusion based on the evidence that you have used.

5. Use evaluative comments based on the information in the sources; this will allow you to make specific, insightful conclusions, e.g. significant increase/decrease, greater than/less than, etc.

TOP TIP

Use different coloured highlighters to help you write your conclusions. Highlight each bullet point a different colour and highlight the information in the sources that matches with each bullet point the same colour. This will help when structuring your answer.

Sample question

Study Sources A, B and C and then attempt the question which follows.

Source A

Social exclusion

Social exclusion is a term used to describe a person or group that lacks sufficient income to play a full part in society. For example, those socially excluded may not have enough money for special celebrations such as birthdays, for toys and books for children or for warm winter clothing. Those people experiencing social exclusion are most likely to be affected by low income, poor health, unemployment, fuel poverty and poor housing. The problems linked with social exclusion are something that both the Scottish and UK governments have been concerned to address in recent years.

Scots are living longer, premature death and crime rates are falling and unemployment rates have also started to fall. However, social exclusion continues to impact on the lives of many Scottish citizens. The wealthiest groups in Scotland continue to lead better lives and the gap between the best and worst off in Scotland continues to widen.

Those who are worst off in Scottish society are less likely to access health services than those who are better off and usually have higher death and illness rates. Low life expectancy rates and long-term illness are often strong indicators of people experiencing social exclusion.

Evidence suggests that those people suffering social exclusion are not equally spread across Scotland. There are significant differences in health, earnings, crime and employment levels between Scottish local authorities and between urban and rural areas.

Source B

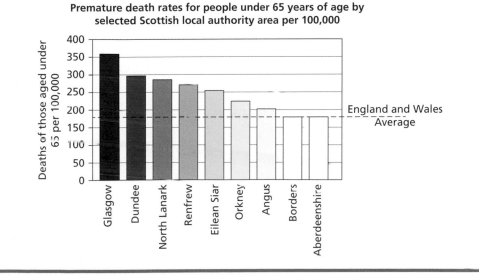

Premature death rates for people under 65 years of age by selected Scottish local authority area per 100,000

Source C

Social and economic data from selected Scottish local authorities

Rural areas	Urban areas
Aberdeenshire	**Dundee City**
• Average gross earnings per week: £570.60	• Average gross earnings per week: £483.30
• Unemployment rate: 1.5%	• Unemployment rate: 5.9%
• Crime rate per 10,000 people: 286	• Crime rate per 10,000 people: 616
• Employment rate: 79.6%	• Employment rate: 68.4%
• Life expectancy: 78.2 years	• Life expectancy: 73.9 years
• Long-standing illness: 11%	• Long-standing illness: 17%
• National percentage share of the poorest parts of the country: 0%	• National percentage share of the poorest parts of the country: 5.8%
Borders	**Glasgow City**
• Average gross earnings per week: £430.11	• Average gross earnings per week: £506
• Unemployment rate: 3.3%	• Unemployment rate: 5.8%
• Crime rate per 10,000 people: 281	• Crime rate per 10,000 people: 889
• Employment rate: 73.1%	• Employment rate: 63.8%
• Life expectancy: 77.5 years	• Life expectancy: 71.6 years
• Long-standing illness: 12%	• Long-standing illness: 22%
• National percentage share of the poorest parts of the country: 0.3%	• National percentage share of the poorest parts of the country: 45%

Attempt the following question using **only** the information in Sources A, B and C above.

What conclusions can be drawn about social exclusion in Scotland?

You must draw conclusions about:

- the links between social exclusion and health.
- the links between social exclusion and local authority area.

You must give an overall conclusion on social exclusion in Scotland. **8 marks**

Sample answer

Links between social exclusion and health

Poor health can be definite evidence of someone experiencing social exclusion. Source A highlights that those who are worst off in society are less likely to access health services than those who are better off, leading to lower life expectancy and higher rates of illness. This is further supported in Source C, which highlights that an area such as Glasgow City houses almost half (45%) of the poorest parts of the country, has almost one-quarter of their population with a long standing illness and the lowest life expectancy of the areas identified, at 71.6 years. Furthermore Source B highlights the link with the number of premature deaths. Glasgow City has a significantly high number of premature deaths, with over 100 more than Aberdeenshire, where none of the poorest parts of the country exist. (3 marks)

Links between social exclusion and local authority area

Those living in local authority areas regarded as urban are more likely to suffer social exclusion than those living in areas regarded as rural. Source A highlights that there are significant differences in health, earnings, crime and employment levels between Scottish local authorities and between urban and rural areas. This is backed up in Source C which highlights that urban areas such as Glasgow City and Dundee have significant differences in unemployment rates, with Glasgow City having a 5.8% unemployment rate and Dundee City having a 5.9% unemployment rate, almost four times that of rural Aberdeenshire where unemployment is a low 1.5%. Social exclusion is also evident in relation to the crime rates. Both areas in Source C identified as rural have less than 300 crimes per 10,000 people whereas the crime rate in Dundee and Glasgow stood at 616 and 889 respectively. Furthermore Source B highlights that those urban areas identified in Source C have the highest rates of premature deaths in comparison to the rural areas identified in Source C, with Dundee having over 100 more premature deaths (approx. 300) per 100,000 people compared to the Borders at less than 200 per 10,000. (3 marks)

Overall conclusion

Overall, the evidence in Sources A, B and C clearly suggests that the factors that lead to social exclusion are strongly linked so that where social exclusion is greatest, health will be poorest. It is also clear that some parts of Scotland suffer more from social exclusion and these are also the local authority areas with the poorest social and economic data. (2 marks)

Detecting and explaining the degree of objectivity

You should be able to use a range of sources of information to detect and explain degrees of objectivity. In the final Exam, this question can occur in **any** section and will be worth 8 marks overall. You will be expected to refer to all sources **as well as** making an overall judgement as to the accuracy of the statement given to gain full marks. It is important to note that as well as marks for statements made and the overall judgement of accuracy, 2 of the 8 marks available can also be awarded for incorporating an evaluation of the reliability of sources used in the question – this is **not** however required to gain full marks.

Steps to success

1. Read the given viewpoint carefully and find the key words – you will use these to identify how objective this view is.

2. Identify which sources or parts of the sources **support** the viewpoint – highlight them one colour.

3. Identify which sources or parts of the sources **oppose** the viewpoint – highlight them another colour. Remember to use **all** the sources – a maximum of only 6 marks will be awarded in the Exam if all sources are not used.

4. Write your answer – remember the key thing is you must interpret and evaluate the sources to detect and explain the degree of objectivity. Up to 3 marks will be awarded for a single detailed objective assessment of the given view, based on the appropriate use of and synthesis of the evidence. The final two marks will be given for an overall judgement on the accuracy of the statement – you cannot achieve full marks without an overall judgment.

5. Use evaluative comments based on the information in the sources, this will allow you to make an overall judgement on the accuracy of the statement – significant increase/decrease, greater than/less than, larger than/smaller than, etc.

Study Sources A and B and then attempt the question which follows.

Source A

Reported crime rate in Scotland falls by 22%

Reported crime in Scotland has fallen by 22% in the past four years according to official figures published in the Scottish Crime and Justice Survey (SCJS).* However, one in six adults in Scotland was the victim of a least one crime in the year to the end of March 2013. The SCJS also reported the risk of crime in Scotland to be lower than that in England and Wales. The risk of being a victim of crime also dropped from 20.4% in 2008–2009 to 16.9% in 2012–2013, a drop described as 'significant' by the report.

Those living in the most deprived areas were more likely to be a victim of crime. Violent crime continues to concern the public and the fear of being the victim of a violent crime such as mugging is increasing. The perceived risk of this is almost 20% higher than the actual risk. In fact, most crime committed in Scotland is property crime, with violent crime being under one-third of all crime in 2012–2013.

Over three-quarters of people surveyed also believed that the level of crime in their area had stayed the same or reduced. The Scottish Justice Secretary said, 'this survey confirms what we already know. Crime is falling, the risk of being a victim of crime is falling and more people are feeling safer in their communities.' He added, 'these statistical trends are consistent with recorded crime statistics which show crime in Scotland is at its lowest level in almost 40 years with the 1000 additional police officers that this government has put in communities protecting the public.'

A Scottish Conservative spokesperson questioned the effectiveness of the survey by saying that many victims of crime did not report it. He said, 'there are a number of areas of concern within these findings. It's clear far too many people are victims of crime, and a significant amount don't even bother reporting it because they don't believe it will be solved.'

Adapted from the BBC website, 7 March, 2014

*The Scottish Crime and Justice Survey (SCJS) is a large-scale continuous survey measuring adults' experiences and perceptions of crime in Scotland. The survey is based on around 12,000 face-to-face interviews with adults (aged 16 and over) living in private households in Scotland.

Source B

Scottish Crime and Justice Survey: % change in estimates of numbers of all crime

Estimated numbers of crimes	2008/09	2010/11	2012/13	% change 2008/09 to 2012/13	% change 2010/11 to 2012/13
ALL SCJS CRIME	1,045,000	874,000	815,000	–22%	–7%
PROPERTY CRIME	728,000	654,000	579,000	–21%	–12%
Vandalism	350,000	275,000	219,000	–37%	–20%
All motor vehicle theft related incidents	70,000	58,000	50,000	–29%	–14%
Housebreaking	25,000	28,000	35,000	+36%	+23%
Other household theft (including bicycles)	173,000	169,000	169,000	–2%	0%
Personal theft (including robbery)	110,000	124,000	106,000	–3%	–14%
VIOLENT CRIME	317,000	220,000	236,000	–25%	+7%
Assault	297,000	208,000	225,000	–24%	+8%
Robbery	20,000	12,000	11,000	–42%	–6%

Attempt the following question using only the information in Sources A and B.

'All kinds of crime have fallen in Scotland.' To what extent is this statement accurate? In your answer you may wish to evaluate the reliability of the sources.

8 marks

Sample answer

Look for key words to help you find evidence to support and oppose.

'All kinds of crime have fallen in Scotland.' To what extent is this statement accurate?

Key words

Evidence to support the statement 'All kinds of crime have fallen in Scotland' is provided in Sources A and B. The Scottish Crime and Justice Survey in Source A highlights that the majority of people surveyed (over three-quarters) believed that the level of crime in their area had remained the same or decreased. This was further supported by the Scottish Justice Secretary identifying that the risk of being a victim of crime is also falling. Source B goes further to support the statement with data that highlights a significant decline in numbers of crimes. Between 2008/09 and 2012/13 crime has fallen by almost one-quarter overall, with some crimes falling by more than one-third, e.g. vandalism (37%) and robbery (42%).

Evaluative comments   **(3 marks)**

Evidence to oppose the statement 'All kinds of crime have fallen in Scotland' is provided in Sources A and B. Source A suggests that the results of the survey may be unreliable given that there are a number of crimes that go unreported due to the victim feeling that the crime will go unsolved. Furthermore Source B opposes the statement in that not ALL crime has fallen. Certain crimes such as housebreaking have significantly increased. Between 2008/09 and 2012/13 housebreaking has increased by more than one-third (36%) and within a more recent period violent crime has also increased indicating that although it has fallen overall, between 2010/11 and 2012/13 it actually increased by 7%.

Evaluative comments   **(3 marks)**

Overall judgment on the accuracy of the statement:

Overall, the evidence **does** support the view. While some crime figures have increased, e.g. housebreaking has gone up by 36%, over the period 2008/09 to 2012/13, the overall figure has fallen by 22% and both property crime and violent crime have fallen by 21% and 25%.

(2 marks)

Note: You can also pick up 2 marks for commenting on the validity, reliability and origin of the sources. This could be helpful if your evidence is not explained/synthesised to the extent that would gain 3 marks.

In the question above it would be suitable to note that:

…the sources of evidence used are reliable as the Scottish Crime and Justice Survey (SCJS) is a large-scale survey of around 12,000 face-to-face interviews. This is a significant sample size and allows for accurate comparisons over a number of years.

Points to consider when examining the reliability and validity of the sources:

- **Date** – is it up to date or out of date?
- **Author** – who created/wrote the source, are they experts/knowledgeable?
- **Bias** – does the source examine both sides of the argument? If the source is a newspaper it might be easy to identify political bias.
- **Sample size** – if the source is based on findings of a survey, consider how many people were surveyed; was it enough to give significant data? Who carried out the survey, are they a recognised, reliable organisation such as Ipsos MORI, YouGov etc?

The Assignment

In order to complete Higher Modern Studies you must undertake an Assignment – you may recall completing something similar in National 5 Modern Studies or other subjects. The Assignment will give you the opportunity to show the application of skills as well as knowledge and is worth 30 marks (33% of the total mark). It is therefore of paramount importance that the Assignment is completed to a high standard.

Your Assignment will be based on a complex contemporary issue that allows for analysis and the application of decision making skills.

Stages

The Assignment has **two** key stages:

1. Research
2. Production of evidence

Research stage

At this initial stage you need to:

- Identify an issue.
- Collect a range of evidence.
- Analyse, evaluate and synthesise information from a range of sources.
- Reach a decision while showing an awareness of alternative viewpoints.

Production of evidence stage

This stage involves writing up your Assignment, under exam conditions, in the format of a report. You will be able to take 'specified resources' into the write-up. The SQA refer to this as **research evidence**. This is evidence you will have collected during the research stage. This evidence should consist of no more than two single-sided sheets of A4 and will be submitted to the SQA with your written report. The research evidence may include:

- Evidence/data from primary or secondary research.
- Bullet points/headings/mind maps.
- Statistical, graphical or numerical data.
- Survey results.
- Interview questions and/or answers.
- Questionnaire and/or results.
- List of internet search engine results.
- Newspaper article or extracts.
- Summary notes taken from a visit or talk/written or audio-visual source.

It is important to remember that your research evidence should be used as a **prompt**. You must **not** simply copy information directly from the research evidence into the Assignment.

Planning the Assignment

In order to achieve the best possible outcome, a high degree of planning and preparation is required.

Selecting your issue for research

Think of the different topics and issues you have looked at in Modern Studies. Create a mind map of the different topics and issues that you could choose to study.

When considering the topic for research think about whether a decision on the topic can be made – the most suitable topics are those where there are a number of possible options or alternatives (courses of action).

Selecting your methods of research and gathering evidence

Your methods of research can be both quantitative and qualitative and can comprise both primary and secondary data (see list on previous page). The methods of research and sources of evidence selected will depend on your chosen topic and the access you have to different methods, however you should aim to have used at least three different methods of research.

Ensure that the information gathered when researching is relevant; note where it originated from on your research evidence sheet. It would be worthwhile selecting five or six sources of information to support you at the production of evidence stage.

It is also worth noting how useful and reliable this information has been as you can gain up to 2 marks for commenting on validity, reliability, bias and the status of the source – official report, statistics, etc.

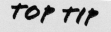

TOP TIP

Remember when using the internet that it comprises a variety of different sources of information: websites, newspaper articles, government reports, blogs, official statistics. Too often candidates refer to research as simply 'using the internet' and give a generic account of the advantages and disadvantages. Ensure that you give specific information regarding which research sources you have used.

Research evidence example

Below are some examples of research evidence gathered for 'Tackling soaring obesity levels in the UK'. A maximum of two sides of A4 should be taken into the write-up stage of the assignment. This should be used as a prompt when writing the assignment up under exam conditions.

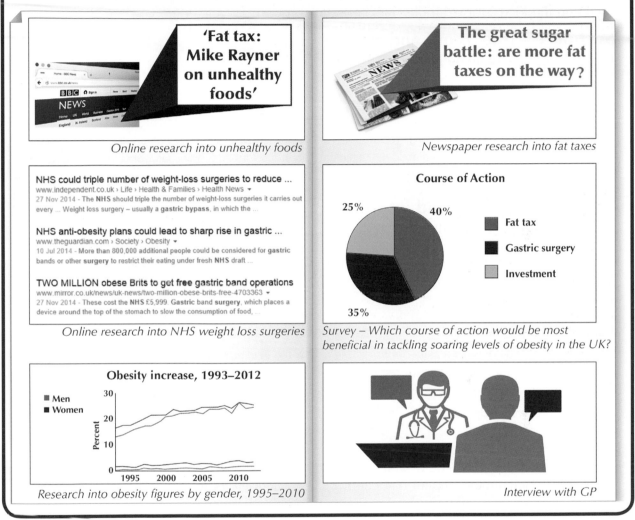

Online research into unhealthy foods

'Fat tax: Mike Rayner on unhealthy foods'

Newspaper research into fat taxes

The great sugar battle: are more fat taxes on the way?

NHS could triple number of weight-loss surgeries to reduce ...
www.independent.co.uk › Life › Health & Families › Health News ▾
27 Nov 2014 - The **NHS** should triple the number of weight-loss surgeries it carries out every ... Weight loss surgery – usually a **gastric bypass**, in which the ...

NHS anti-obesity plans could lead to sharp rise in gastric ...
www.theguardian.com › Society › Obesity ▾
10 Jul 2014 - More than 800,000 additional people could be considered for **gastric** bands or other **surgery** to restrict their eating under fresh **NHS** draft ...

TWO MILLION obese Brits to get free gastric band operations
www.mirror.co.uk/news/uk-news/two-million-obese-brits-free-4703363 ▾
27 Nov 2014 - These cost the **NHS** £5,999. **Gastric** band **surgery**, which places a device around the top of the stomach to slow the consumption of food, ...

Online research into NHS weight loss surgeries

Course of Action

- 25%
- 40%
- 35%

Fat tax
Gastric surgery
Investment

Survey – Which course of action would be most beneficial in tackling soaring levels of obesity in the UK?

Obesity increase, 1993–2012

- Men
- Women

Research into obesity figures by gender, 1995–2010

Interview with GP

Writing the report

Given that the Assignment is worth 30 marks, it is crucial that you understand where these marks come from. They are broken down as follows:

- Knowledge and understanding of the issue/alternative courses of action – 10 marks
- Use of sources to support your arguments/recommendations (analysis/synthesis) – 10 marks
- Structure (report format) – 4 marks
- Evaluation of sources (validity, reliability, bias) – 2 marks
- Overall decision/conclusion – 4 marks

Possible structure for 'report format' Assignment

Title

Begin with the title; you could use your surname, for example, 'The Allardyce Report' and then add the focus, for example 'Tackling soaring obesity levels in the UK'.

Section 1 – role, remit and responsibility

Identify the issue that you have chosen to research. Give an explanation as to why this topic is relevant:

My name is Dianne Allardyce and I am a health policy advisor. I have been tasked by the UK government to undertake significant research with a focus on addressing the soaring levels of obesity in the UK. It is clear that there are three potential courses of action and on conclusion of this research I aim to make a clear recommendation to the UK government on which course of action is most suitable to address this issue.

Section 2 – background information

This should be background information relating to the problem. In this case, statistics to highlight the growth in obesity in adults and children, links to health and wealth inequalities, links to the variety of killer diseases, long-term impact on health, costs to the NHS, etc.

Potential courses of action:

- *'Fat tax' – introduction of a surcharge on fattening foods and drinks.*
- *'Investment in education' – increased funding of education programmes in schools to promote healthy living and lifestyles.*
- *'Gastric surgery' – resources provided to accommodate further gastric surgery procedures on those regarded as morbidly obese – short-term cost to give a long-term gain.*

Sections 3–5

Sections 3–5 will outline the arguments for and against your potential courses of action. You should indicate the impact that each course of action would have on certain areas of society, e.g. government and opposition parties, taxation, social policy, human rights, relationships with other countries, etc.

You must synthesise between sources and where possible use evaluative language (remember to annotate your margin where you have made reference to specific sources of evidence on your research evidence sheet).

Section 3 – 'fat tax'

Outline the arguments to support your recommendation:

3.1

3.2

3.3

Outline the arguments against your recommendation:

3.4

3.5

3.6

Section 4 – 'investment in education'

Outline the arguments to support your recommendation:

4.1

4.2

4.3

Outline the arguments against your recommendation:

4.4

4.5

4.6

Section 5 – 'gastric surgery'

Outline the arguments to support your recommendation:

5.1

5.2

5.3

Outline the arguments against your recommendation:

5.4

5.5

5.6

Section 6 – conclusion

Make a decision – use your knowledge and understanding of the issue and your analysis of it to make a decision about what the best courses of action would be in this situation.

Section 7 – methodologies

Evaluation of the usefulness and reliability of the sources of information you have used on your research evidence sheet.

The UK political system

The UK constitutional arrangement

The UK has no formal written constitution, that is, no single document where laws, rules and practices on how the state is governed is set out. As a result the UK is often referred to as having an 'uncodified' constitution – in that there is no single reference source. However this is misleading in that the governing laws and practices of the UK are written in a variety of documents: statute law (Acts of Parliament), EU law and ruling judgements from court decisions, and the constitutional arrangement highlights clearly the different branches of government and their respective roles and functions.

The diagram below appears to show that the monarch is the most powerful branch, however over time the power once held by the monarch has been attributed to parliament. This is often referred to as 'parliamentary sovereignty'. Parliamentary sovereignty ensures that the UK Parliament has overall legal authority, which means it has the power to devise, amend or terminate any law. However, the diagram below also highlights the changes to parliamentary sovereignty in recent years, i.e. the creation of devolved bodies, with the transfer of significant powers to the Scottish Parliament, the Welsh Assembly and the Northern Ireland Assembly. Furthermore, parliamentary sovereignty has been limited as a result of political change both inside and outside the UK.

The Queen – Head of State

David Cameron – PM
Head of Government
Executive Branch

MPs/Lords
House of Commons/Lords
Legislative Branch

Devolved Bodies – MSPs
The Scottish Parliament
(Devolved Matters)

Supreme Court
Judges
Judicial Branch

The UK constitutional arrangement

TOP TIP

Use the following link to identify further evidence of developments that have affected parliamentary sovereignty: www.parliament.uk/about/how/sovereignty

The monarch is still regarded as Head of State, however her role in parliament is clearly viewed as one of carrying out traditional and ceremonial functions, including appointing the Prime Minister, dissolving parliament and delivering the speech marking the beginning of the parliamentary year. However, we must understand fully what each of the other branches does.

State opening of parliament

The branches of the UK constitutional arrangement

Executive branch (Prime Minister and cabinet)

The Prime Minister is head of the UK government. He is ultimately responsible for all policy and decisions. He oversees the operation of the Civil Service and government agencies, appoints members of the government and is the key government figure in the House of Commons.

Legislative branch (House of Commons and House of Lords)

This branch of the constitutional arrangement examines and challenges the work of the government – this is called scrutiny. It debates and discusses government policy, proposed legislation and current issues. It approves and passes all new laws and it therefore enables the government to raise taxes.

Judicial branch (Courts)

This branch is responsible for interpreting the law and deciding on legal disputes.

Devolved bodies: Scottish Parliament, Welsh Assembly, Northern Ireland Assembly

Takes responsibility for devolved powers. Devolved powers are decisions that the UK Parliament controlled in the past. This could include matters like education or health.

Quick Test

1. Describe what is meant by the term 'uncodified constitution'.
2. Explain, in detail, the importance of parliamentary sovereignty.
3. Using the website from the Top Tip, list three further laws that affected parliamentary sovereignty.
4. Summarise the roles and functions of each of the branches of government: executive, legislative and judicial.

The role and powers of UK central government

Government and **parliament** are often confused with one another. They do however, work closely together as they both play a part in forming the laws of the United Kingdom. However, they are separate institutions with separate functions.

Government	Parliament
The government runs the country. It has responsibility for developing and implementing policy and for drafting laws. It is also known as the 'executive'.	Parliament is the highest legislative authority in the UK. It has responsibility for checking the work of the government and examining, debating and approving new laws. It is also known as the 'legislature'.

Forming a government

The political party that wins an overall majority in the House of Commons after a general election forms the new government and by consequence the party leader becomes the Prime Minister (PM). In 2015, the Conservative Party had the majority of seats with 331 and as a result David Cameron became Prime Minister for a second term. However, when no one single party wins a majority of seats the largest party may form a minority government or there may be a coalition government formed, as was the case in 2010 when the Conservative Party joined with the Liberal Democrats, with David Cameron becoming the Prime Minister and Nick Clegg, the leader of the Liberal Democrats, his Deputy. The Prime Minister then has the task of appointing ministers who work in the government departments; the most senior of these ministers sit in the Cabinet.

The role of the Prime Minister

The Prime Minister is head of the UK government. He or she is ultimately responsible for all policy and decisions, providing political leadership and the political direction to be taken by the government, setting key priorities and strategies. The PM oversees the operation of the Civil Service and government agencies, appoints members of the Cabinet and is the principal government figure in the House of Commons.

Powers of the PM

Patronage

This is the power to appoint someone to an important position. The PM can appoint Cabinet ministers, initiate Cabinet reshuffles, appoint life peers and make recommendations within the honours system. For example, David Cameron appointed Michael Gove as Justice Secretary in May 2015, after Chris Grayling became Leader of the House.

Authority within the Cabinet system

The PM chairs the Cabinet meetings and manages their agenda, that is, their length and frequency, as well as directing and summing up the Cabinet discussion.

David Cameron

Party leadership – the leader of the largest party in the House of Commons

A large working majority can strengthen the power of the PM as the governing party is able to deliver its manifesto and policy commitments with ease. David Cameron, during the coalition, often had to rely on the support of the Liberal Democrats in order to pass legislation, e.g. welfare reforms. However, with a majority of MPs in the House of the Commons following the 2015 general election, he should see his power return.

Public standing – high public profile

The Prime Minister provides political leadership at home and represents the UK on the international stage. He or she has regular discussions with other world leaders and attends formal meetings of heads of state: EU, G20 summits and the UN. David Cameron spoke about addressing climate change through global action at the UN Climate Summit 2014.

Policy-making

The PM's power to influence policy is not limited to one area – the Prime Minister has the ability to get involved across all areas of responsibility, especially areas where there is a particular interest. David Cameron has taken a keen interest in welfare reform and in September 2014 unveiled quite radical plans to reduce youth unemployment. However during the coalition Cameron was limited by the Liberal Democrats and has been defeated on particular issues such as the EU. Even with a majority post-2015 he may be limited due to the vast number of SNP MPs who are able to force delays in Commons votes, as was the case over fox hunting.

Role and powers of government

A Cabinet meeting

Government departments and their agencies are responsible for putting government policy into practice. Some departments, like the Ministry of Defence, cover the whole of the UK. Others don't – the Department of Health doesn't cover Scotland, Wales and Northern Ireland as this matter is devolved to their respective parliament and assemblies.

The government, i.e. the Prime Minister and government ministers, is supported by the Civil Service. The Civil Service is politically neutral and must serve the government of the day, regardless of the party in power. The Civil Service is responsible for the practical and administrative work of the government. PMs will often also use special advisors who are sometimes referred to as 'spin doctors'. They are often viewed as manipulating information in order to preserve the reputation of the PM or the government.

TOP TIP

For further information on the role and powers of UK central government visit gov.uk: www.gov.uk/government/how-government-works

Quick Test

1. Outline the difference between government and parliament.
2. Explain how the government is formed.
3. Why does government not have full responsibility for all policy areas in the UK?

The role and powers of the devolved bodies

The devolution process throughout the late 1990s led to the creation of a separate Parliament in Scotland and a National Assembly in both Wales and Northern Ireland. The process gave the decision making bodies the **power to legislate** on **devolved matters**, often areas where regional differences exist, while Westminster retained control of **reserved matters** – areas that affect the UK as a whole or those with an international element.

Scottish Parliament

The Scottish Parliament building in Edinburgh

The Scotland Act 1998 was the initial Act of the UK Parliament that passed powers to legislate on devolved matters. These powers were extended by the Scotland Act of 2012.

Devolved matters	Reserved matters
✓ Agriculture, forestry and fisheries	✗ Benefits and social security
✓ Education and training	✗ Immigration
✓ Environment	✗ Defence
✓ Health and social services	✗ Foreign policy
✓ Housing	✗ Employment
✓ Law and order (including the licensing of air weapons)	✗ Broadcasting
✓ Local government	✗ Trade and industry
✓ Sport and the arts	✗ Nuclear energy, oil, coal, gas and electricity
✓ Tourism and economic development	✗ Consumer rights
✓ Many aspects of transport	✗ Data protection
	✗ The Constitution

The Scottish Parliament also has the power to vary the UK rate of income tax by 3p, however they have never used it. The Scotland Act 2012 outlines further matters to be transferred to the Scottish Parliament. Some of these have now been devolved, for example the power to legislate over regulations on drink-driving and speed limits. Further matters are guaranteed to be transferred after the failed bid for independence in 2014. What these matters will be and when they will be transferred is still being negotiated.

TOP TIP

The Scotland Act lists the matters that are reserved to the UK Parliament in Schedule 5 – if the matter is not listed in this section, it is devolved to the Scottish Parliament.

The Scottish Parliament can however ask the UK government to legislate on devolved matters that they may be considering for England – this is known as a Legislative Consent Motion, sometimes referred to as Sewel Motions. In certain circumstances it can be sensible and advantageous for Scotland to be included in a Westminster bill that refers to a devolved matter, for example in May 2012 the Scottish Parliament agreed relevant points in the Crime and Courts Bill passed at Westminster in relation to the Proceeds of Crime.

Welsh Assembly and Northern Ireland Assembly

The Northern Ireland Assembly building

Like the Scottish Parliament, the Assemblies have power to legislate on a number of areas. The Welsh Assembly held its first election in 1999, while the Northern Ireland Assembly had held its first election the year before (in June 1998). However, the Northern Ireland Assembly has been suspended on occasion with power returning to Westminster.

Welsh Assembly devolved matters	Northern Ireland Assembly devolved matters
• Agriculture, fisheries, forestry and rural development • Ancient monuments and historic buildings • Culture • Economic development • Education and training • The environment • Fire and rescue services and the promotion of fire safety • Food • Health and health services • Highways and transport • Housing • Local government • Public administration • Social welfare • Sport and recreation • Tourism • Town and country planning • Water and flood defence • The Welsh language	• Health and social services • Education • Employment and skills • Agriculture • Social security • Pensions and child support • Housing • Economic development • Local government • Environmental issues, including planning • Transport • Culture and sport • The Northern Ireland Civil Service • Equal opportunities • Justice and policing

More recently the Welsh Assembly has launched a consultation in a bid for tax raising powers – the first piece of Welsh tax legislation since 1283. The White Paper proposes the creation of the Welsh Revenue Authority, which would be responsible for the collection and management of Welsh taxes. Furthermore, there have been suggestions that the Political and Constitutional Affairs Select Committee will examine extending some powers that have been transferred to Scotland to the rest of the UK.

The logo of the Welsh Assembly

Quick Test

1. Outline the difference between a devolved and reserved matter.
2. Which power does the Scottish Parliament have that neither of the Assemblies has?
3. Have a look at the information on this website and outline what the 'Hillsborough Agreement' is: http://education.niassembly.gov.uk/post_16/snapshots_of_devolution/activity

The impact of EU membership on decision making in the UK

The UK joined the European Union (EU) in 1972 and as a member state agrees to abide by decisions taken and laws implemented by the EU. EU laws, in the form of regulations, decisions and directives, take precedence over UK laws and have to be accepted as legally binding. The EU also issues non-binding laws that are viewed as recommendations or suggestions and can be incorporated into national law or not. David Cameron however has pledged to hold an in-or-out referendum by May 2017, which could see the UK leave the EU.

The EU building in Brussels

EU impact on UK citizens

In recent years EU decisions have affected our jobs, family life and the environment. Members of the European Parliament (MEPs) have passed laws on the cost of texting from abroad, the use of energy-efficient light bulbs and the prevention of budget airlines from using misleading adverts such as 'flights for 50p'. The EU have also ensured fair treatment in the judicial system for all EU citizens. The European Arrest Warrant means that you can be arrested in any EU country for a serious crime that has been committed anywhere in the EU.

Certain EU directives have been criticised here in the UK. The European Working Time Directive – giving workers rights to rest time and minimum holiday entitlement – has been criticised by health unions as it means that junior doctors are unable to work beyond 48 hours per week, which is seen as damaging to the amount of training they receive. Some UK MPs have suggested that leaving the EU would benefit the UK with regard to decision making.

EU law/UK law

A recent decision by the EU Employment Appeal Tribunal highlighted EU law becoming more powerful than UK law. Two Moroccan women had been sacked by diplomatic missions (working in the embassies of foreign states) in the UK and were claiming unfair dismissal on the grounds of unpaid wages and breaches of working time regulations. Both claims were initially dismissed on the grounds that foreign embassies gain immunity from the jurisdiction of UK courts. However, their legal team was able to proceed with the case under EU law in relation to the Working Time Directive.

However there are times when EU decisions are in direct contrast to UK law – a clear example being the UK ban on prisoners gaining the right to vote. The European Court of Human Rights states that this ban is a clear breach of the human rights of the prisoner; however the Human Rights Act (1998) stipulates that their decisions only need be taken 'into account'.

Members of the European Parliament cast a vote

TOP TIP

Use this link to learn more about EU law:
http://ec.europa.eu/atwork/applying-eu-law/index_en.htm

Quick Test

1. Using the Top Tip link above, give definitions for regulations, directives and decisions.
2. List three examples of how EU law has impacted on our everyday lives.
3. Which EU law has caused controversy in the UK in recent years? Explain why this has been the case.

The Independence Referendum

Since the creation of the Scottish Parliament in 1999 the SNP has continually called for a referendum on independence, their flagship policy – allowing the public to vote on whether to remain as part of the UK or move to become a separate country. The Scotland Act (2012) had already transferred further power to the Scottish Parliament and in December 2013 the Scottish Referendum Act was given royal assent,

> *'to make provision, in accordance with paragraph 5A of Part 1 of Schedule 5 to the Scotland Act 1998, for the holding of a referendum in Scotland on a question about the independence of Scotland.'*

The referendum of September 2014

Both 'Yes Scotland' and 'Better Together' put forward comprehensive campaigns outlining the benefits and consequences of voting yes or no in the referendum and two days prior to the vote all three leaders of the main UK political parties united in a 'vow' to deliver 'faster, safer and better change' for Scotland should Scotland vote no. In the final days prior to the referendum polling organisations found it too close to call and on the day the result ended 55% No to 45% Yes. Immediately Alex Salmond, then Scotland's First Minister, urged the unionist parties to deliver more powers to the Scottish Parliament with Prime Minister David Cameron expressing his delight at the result, ensuring that the three main unionist parties at Westminster would follow through with their 'pledge' of more powers. Lord Smith of Kelvin was appointed to oversee the process of further transfer of power, including new powers relating to taxation, spending and welfare. David Cameron also announced that the controversial 'West Lothian question' would be dealt with.

THE VOW

The people of Scotland want to know that all three main parties will deliver change for Scotland.

WE ARE AGREED THAT:

The Scottish Parliament is permanent and extensive new powers for the Parliament will be delivered by the process and to the timetable agreed and announced by our three parties, starting on 19th September.

And it is our hope that the people of Scotland will be engaged directly as each party works to improve the way we are governed in the UK in the years ahead.

We agree that the UK exists to ensure opportunity and security for all by sharing our resources equitably across all four nations to secure the defence, prosperity and welfare of every citizen.

And because of the continuation of the Barnett allocation for resources, and the powers of the Scottish Parliament to raise revenue, we can state categorically that the final say on how much is spent on the NHS will be a matter for the Scottish Parliament.

We believe that the arguments that so powerfully make the case for staying together in the UK should underpin our future as a country. We will honour those principles and values not only before the referendum but after.

People want to see change. A No vote will deliver faster, safer and better change than separation.

David Cameron   Ed Miliband   Nick Clegg

The vow made by the three UK party leaders

powers relating to taxation, spending and welfare. David Cameron also announced that the controversial 'West Lothian question' would be dealt with.

Lord Smith published his report setting out the agreement that had been reached by the five main political parties in the Scottish Parliament on 27 November, 2014. Lord Smith acknowledged that 'compromise' had been key in achieving this agreement, with some parties accepting a move to devolve greater powers than had originally been anticipated, while others had to accept that certain elements of the agreement fell short of their expectations.

Overall, the recommendations of the report aimed to create a 'coherent set of powers that strengthen the Scottish Parliament's ability to pursue its own vision, goals and objectives, whatever they might be at any particular time', with the recommendations setting out 'the biggest transfer of power to the Scottish Parliament since its establishment'.

Key recommendations

The Smith Commission's report set out the following recommendations.

Lord Smith with the report

- The Scottish Government will receive all **income tax** paid by Scottish taxpayers on their income with an adjustment made to the block grant received from the UK government as a result – an adapted Barnett formula will continue to be used to determine the block grant.

- Scotland will be given power over **air passenger duty**.

- MSPs will have **control over elections** to both the Scottish Parliament and Scottish local authorities, as well as provision to be made to allow the Scottish Parliament to rule on whether **16- and 17-year-olds will be able to vote** in both of these elections.

- Scottish Ministers should be wholly involved in agreeing any UK position in **EU negotiations relating to devolved matters**.

- **Broadcasting** – the BBC will submit an annual report to the Scottish Parliament and appear before Scottish Parliament committees should the need arise in the same way it does in the UK Parliament.

- **Welfare** – the Scottish Parliament will have the power to vary the housing element of universal credit payments (this will allow MSPs to cancel the under-occupancy charge, which has been dubbed the 'bedroom tax' by its critics) and will also have the power to create new welfare benefits in devolved areas.

- **Oil and gas** – the licensing of onshore oil and gas extraction underlying Scotland will be devolved to the Scottish Parliament. The licensing of offshore oil and gas extraction will remain reserved.

> **TOP TIP**
> To view the full report published by the Smith Commission use the following link: www.smith-commission.scot

David Cameron met with Nicola Sturgeon in May 2015 and stated that he would be open to 'sensible suggestions' with regard to transferring further powers, especially in relation to welfare.

Quick Test

1. Explain what you understand 'the pledge' or 'the vow' to mean.
2. Outline why Lord Smith acknowledged that 'compromise' had occurred when reaching an agreement on the recommendations to be made.
3. Summarise the key recommendations of the report published by the Smith Commission.

Representative democracy in the UK

Democracy = Rule by the People

The UK is a representative democracy: UK citizens elect representatives to make decisions on their behalf. In the UK we elect a number of representatives, e.g. MPs, MSPs, MEPs and local councillors. These representatives work for us in their respective parliaments and committees and remain in post until the electorate vote them out of office or they resign.

Advantages of representative democracy

- Practical form of participation.
- Ordinary citizens do not have the constant responsibility of decision making.
- Governments should consist of interested, knowledgeable members with relevant experience.

Referenda

UK citizens can however still be consulted on major decisions through a referendum (a vote on a single issue), for example the referendum in 2014 on whether Scotland would become an independent country, or the UK-wide referendum in 2011 on whether or not the country would change its voting system for general elections from First Past The Post to the Alternative Vote system.

Democracy in the UK

UK citizens vote every five years to elect MPs who will represent us in the House of Commons, discussing and debating matters and voting on bills that may or may not become law. By electing a Member of Parliament we are giving over our power to a representative, ultimately withdrawing from the decision making process. If we are content with our MP in the House of Commons we continue to elect them for a number of years – Tam Dalyell was first elected to the House of Commons in 1962 and served continuously until 2005. As the longest serving MP, he was known as the 'Father of the House'.

Tam Dalyell

Democracy in Scotland

In Scotland, elections to the Scottish Parliament take place every four years – so far in 1999, 2003, 2007 and 2011 – with 129 MSPs elected to represent the people of Scotland. The next election however will take place in May 2016 due to the fact that the UK general election took place in 2015. This is due to an agreement that elections using different electoral systems should not occur on the same day. Former Deputy Prime Minister Nick Clegg offered the Scottish Parliament the right to vary the election date by one year either way. The offer was accepted and 2016 given as the chosen date.

The Scottish Parliament

Quick Test

1. In which way do the majority of citizens participate in a representative democracy?
2. List the advantages of a representative democracy.
3. Why is the next Scottish Parliament election taking place in 2016, instead of 2015?

Role and influence of MPs

MPs are elected by the UK electorate to represent their interests and concerns in the House of Commons. MPs are involved in considering and proposing new laws, and can use their position to ask government ministers questions about current issues.

MPs divide their time between working in the parliament, in their constituency and for their political party. Constituents can contact their MP in a number of ways to try to gain their support, including visiting their MP's surgery, lobbying them in parliament or by email or telephone.

An MP's constituency office

Influence in parliament

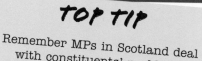

TOP TIP

Remember MPs in Scotland deal with constituents' problems around **reserved** matters only.

MPs have a number of opportunities to influence decision making in parliament, holding the government to account, while working on behalf of their constituents.

Prime Minister's Question Time

Each Wednesday the PM takes questions in the House of Commons for 30 minutes. This allows backbenchers (MPs who hold no governmental office) to ask questions on behalf of their constituents. In most cases, the session starts with a routine 'open question' from an MP about the Prime Minister's engagements. MPs can then ask supplementary questions on any subject, often one of current political significance. Opposition MPs follow up on this or another topic, usually led by the Leader of the Opposition. Usually, he or she is the only MP allowed to come back with further questions. Examples of typical question topics include equality, parliamentary reform and spending cuts.

Question Time

Question Time in the House of Commons is an opportunity for MPs to question government ministers about matters for which they are responsible. Question Time takes place in the first hour of business each day.

Debating

Frequently, issues concerning the country will be debated at length. MPs can contribute to such debates, particularly if they are of direct concern to their constituents. Issues such as firearms, immigration, terrorism, and the NHS are often debated on the floor of the House of Commons.

Adjournment debates

The half-hour adjournment debate offers another opportunity for MPs to raise matters. Usually taken as the last business of the day, MPs must either win a ballot or be chosen by the Speaker to voice their concern. MPs can also raise matters in debates in Westminster Hall. These are similar to adjournment debates in the Chamber but take place on Tuesdays and Wednesdays and may last for either half an hour or an hour and a half.

Voting

MPs are often required to vote on the passing of legislation or decisions relating to international issues. In September 2014 David Cameron recalled parliament to vote on whether the UK would join France and the US in airstrikes on Islamic State militants in Iraq. How your MP votes in parliament may determine whether you continue to support them or not. This link allows you to find your local MP and see how they voted on key issues: www.theyworkforyou.com

Select Committees

These committees check and report on areas ranging from the work of government departments to economic affairs. The results of these inquiries are public and many require a response from the government. The Home Affairs Committee have recently held high profile inquiries into the police, the media and criminal investigations.

Private Members' Bills

An MP might introduce a Private Members' Bill in an attempt to pass a new law. Each year 20 MPs are selected from a ballot and are given the opportunity to bring their own bill forward and have it debated in parliament. Some MPs might use it as an opportunity to highlight a controversial issue, while others might want to make a small change to the law. For example in 2012 Sir Paul Beresford, MP, introduced the Prisons (Interference with Wireless Telegraphy) Act 2012, which allows prison governors to block mobile phone signals, to prevent inmates from carrying out illegal activities while imprisoned. However, few of these bills are successful because of time constraints and the support required from other MPs.

Pressures faced by MPs

It may appear that MPs have significant opportunities to influence the decision making process, however it is evident that there are a number of limits to the amount of influence they have. Any of these factors may limit an MP's influence:

- Time
- Local interests
- The national interest
- Personal conscience
- The party whip
- Pressure groups
- Professional lobbyists
- Constituents

Quick Test

1. Between which aspects of their job must an MP divide his or her time?
2. Select three ways an MP can gain influence in the decision making process. Outline why each would be beneficial.
3. Use your class notes and discussions, and further research, to identify why an MP might find the following limits an issue: time, the party whip, professional lobbyists.

Role of the executive and legislature in the UK

The UK is referred to as a parliamentary government and as both the executive and legislature work closely together they can often be confused with one another.

Key features of parliamentary government

A Cabinet meeting

- **Executive and legislature membership overlaps** – the Prime Minister and members of the Cabinet are also Members of Parliament.

- **Legislature can remove the executive** – the government is accountable to parliament and should there be extreme conflict between the two, parliament can propose a vote of no confidence. Prior to 2011 the Prime Minister could dissolve parliament by calling a general election, usually when he or she was most confident of winning the election. However, the Fixed Term Parliament Act was passed on 15 September, 2011, providing for general elections to be held on the first Thursday in May every five years.

- **Elections to parliament lead to the formation of the government** – a political party that wins an overall majority in the House of Commons at a general election forms the new government and its leader becomes Prime Minister. If no party wins a majority of the seats then the largest party may form a minority government or there may be a coalition government of two or more parties. The Prime Minister appoints ministers who work in the government departments; the most senior of these sit in Cabinet.

Forming an Executive

A political party that wins an overall majority in the House of Commons at a general election forms the new government and its leader becomes Prime Minister. If no party wins a majority of the seats then the largest party may form a minority government or there may be a coalition government of two or more parties as was the case after 2010 when the Conservatives formed a coalition with the Liberal Democrats. The Prime Minister appoints ministers who work in the government departments, the most senior of these sit in the Cabinet. This affords the Prime Minister a significant amount of power – 'hire and fire' – David Cameron appointed Michael Gove as Minister for Education in 2010, however demoted him to Chief Whip in 2014.

Ministers and MPs

Government ministers are chosen from MPs and Lords in Parliament. Ministers must regularly respond to oral and written questions from MPs and Lords as part of the government being held accountable for their actions. In June 2015 questions were taken in the House of Commons by a number of ministers including those responsible for energy and climate change, international development and defence. You can see a timetable of upcoming questions here: www.parliament.uk/documents/commons-table-office/order-of-oral-questions1.pdf

Scrutiny of the government

Parliament checks the work of the government on behalf of UK citizens through investigative Select Committees and by asking government ministers questions. The House of Commons also has to approve proposals for government taxes and spending.

Government bills

Each year the government informs parliament of its plans for new legislation in the Queen's Speech. New legislation is usually introduced in the form of a bill that must be debated and approved by parliament before it can become an Act of Parliament – the government needs the support of the majority of the House of Commons to function.

If a government has a small majority or is working in a coalition they may rely on MPs from other parties supporting the bill. Otherwise the government may face defeat and the bill will fail.

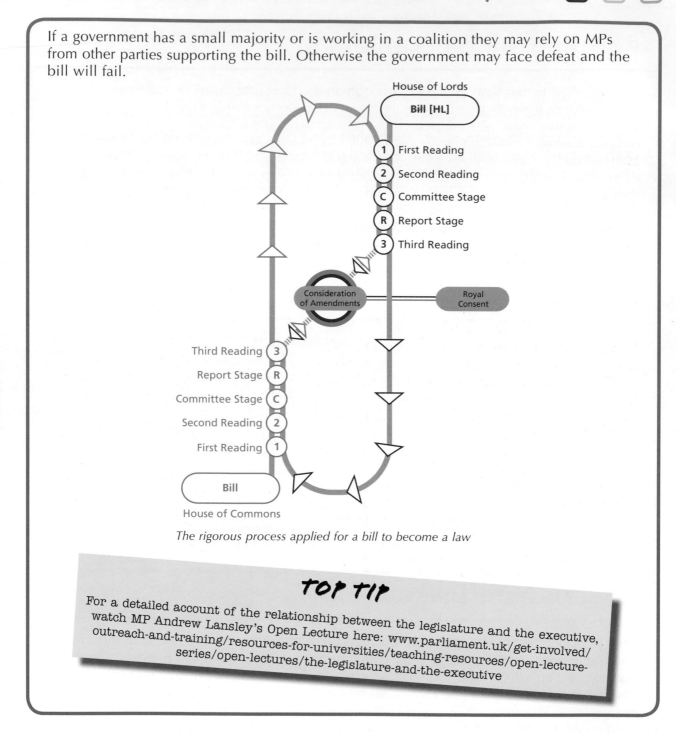

The rigorous process applied for a bill to become a law

TOP TIP

For a detailed account of the relationship between the legislature and the executive, watch MP Andrew Lansley's Open Lecture here: www.parliament.uk/get-involved/outreach-and-training/resources-for-universities/teaching-resources/open-lecture-series/open-lectures/the-legislature-and-the-executive

Quick Test

1.	Why is it correct to suggest that the executive and legislature 'overlap'?
2.	What two problems do winning political parties face when forming a government, if they have no majority after a general election?
3.	List three difficulties that the executive faces when introducing new legislation.

The Scottish Parliament

The role and influence of MSPs

When the Scottish Parliament was established in 1999 it was founded on the principles of sharing power, accountability, access and participation and equal opportunities. The role and influence of MSPs in the Scottish Parliament go some way to ensuring that these principles are upheld. However at times the influence that MSPs have could be said to be limited.

MSPs are able to debate and vote on relevant and current devolved matters. They are also able to debate and discuss reserved matters but they are unable to make any amendments to laws regarding these matters.

First Minister's Question Time (FMQT)

FMQT is held each Thursday for 30 minutes and MSPs are given the opportunity to question the First Minister on specific, current topics and hold him or her to account for the actions taken by the government. The FM in this situation has to outline/justify the policy plans, proposals and decisions of the government. The influence MSPs can have however is limited by the time – 30 minutes only allows for a small number of questions and furthermore the first two questions are afforded to the leaders of the Labour and Conservative parties. There have been times when not all six questions tabled have been asked, causing frustration for backbench MSPs.

First Minister's Question Time

Question Time/Themed Question Time

Question Time is held once each week allowing members the opportunity to direct questions to any member of the Scottish Government. Themed Question Time gives MSPs the opportunity to ask questions on a particular theme, so long as it is a devolved matter. It allows members to scrutinise the government and ministers responsible for certain departments. Furthermore it allows MSPs the chance to ask questions on behalf of their constituents. However MSPs are entered into a ballot in order to ask a question and are randomly selected by the Presiding Officer. All questions are submitted beforehand in order for ministers to prepare an answer. The final constraint here is that there are usually 10–20 questions on the agenda but MSPs are faced with the issue of time once again, with QT given 20 minutes and TQT given 40 minutes.

Members' Bills

MSPs can introduce a Member's Bill with the aim of it becoming law. Each MSP has the opportunity to introduce two bills per parliamentary session and requires the support of 11 other MSPs. The Presiding Officer decides if the proposed bill falls within the remit of the Scottish Parliament and, once accepted, it must be treated like an Executive Bill, going through the three stages for passing such legislation. There are limits to how much influence an MSP can have in this area due to the fact that they may require the support of opposition parties to move the bill to the second stage.

Case study – Control of Dogs Bill

The Control of Dogs (Scotland) Act came into force in 2010 as a result of a Member's Bill introduced by Christine Graham MSP. The new law aims to judge dogs on their behaviour, rather than breed, and gives powers to impose penalties on irresponsible owners.

Committees

Committees play a central part in the work of the parliament and have often been regarded as its 'engine room'. Committees are cross-party, set their own priorities, independent of government, and are responsible for scrutinising legislation, taking evidence from witnesses and conducting inquiries. Committees can request members of the Scottish Government to attend and give evidence on specific areas of concern, along with members of the public, specialist organisations or pressure groups. Furthermore they look at the need for new legislation and MSPs are able to establish a committee on a short-term basis to consider particular issues –

Donald Trump giving evidence to the Economy, Energy and Tourism Committee

Private Bill Committees look at a particular bill that has been introduced by an MSP. Committees are often asked to review petitions passed from the Petitions Committee if the matter falls into their jurisdiction, for example the Education Committee was asked to consider a petition submitted by the Educational Institute of Scotland (EIS) on jobs for new teachers. Finally, committees can propose their own bills to parliament; some have been very successful, ultimately becoming law.

Quick Test

1. List the founding principles of the Scottish Parliament.
2. Outline how an MSP can exert influence with regard to introducing a Member's Bill. Give evidence to support your answer.
3. Use the Scottish Parliament website at: www.scottish.parliament.uk/visitandlearn/44300.aspx to outline the constraints an MSP faces with regard to influence in the committee system.

The Scottish Government

After a Scottish Parliament election, a First Minister is formally nominated by the elected members of the Scottish Parliament and appointed by the Queen, in her capacity as Head of State. Once appointed, the First Minister appoints Scottish government ministers in order to establish a Cabinet, responsible for the different areas devolved to the Scottish Parliament.

First Minister

Since the creation of the Scottish Parliament, Scotland has had five First Ministers.

1. Donald Dewar, May 1999 – October 2000
2. Henry McLeish, October 2000 – November 2001
3. Jack McConnell, November 2001 – May 2007
4. Alex Salmond, May 2007 – November 2014
5. Nicola Sturgeon, November 2014 – present

Alex Salmond and Nicola Sturgeon

Role and powers of the First Minister

The role and powers of the First Minister are set out in Sections 45 to 49 of the Scotland Act 1998.

- To lead the Scottish Government – Alex Salmond was fortunate in his second term as FM as he had an overall majority of MSPs in the Scottish Parliament and was able to pass legislation without relying heavily on other parties, unlike Labour in the first two sessions between 1999 and 2007, when a coalition was formed with the Liberal Democrats.

- To nominate ministers to sit in the Scottish Cabinet and junior ministers to form the Scottish Government. They can also remove them from office. In 2012 Alex Salmond reshuffled the Cabinet to place Nicola Sturgeon at the heart of the bid for independence, moving Alex Neil to Health. In 2009 we witnessed the demotion of Fiona Hyslop from Education Secretary to Culture and External Affairs Minister.
- Responsible to the Scottish Parliament for his/her actions and the actions of the overall Scottish Government.
- Responsible for the development, implementation and presentation of government policy, constitutional affairs and promoting and representing Scotland.
- Delivering oral statements to the Scottish Parliament – at the beginning of each parliamentary term the FM is able to deliver the government's priorities for the forthcoming term.

The Scottish Government

The Scottish Government is the executive branch of the devolved government of Scotland and operates on the basis of collective responsibility. This means that all decisions reached by ministers, individually or collectively, are binding on all members of the government. Furthermore the Scottish Government is accountable (answerable) to the Scottish Parliament.

There are nine Cabinet Secretaries (Cabinet Ministers) including the First Minister, and 10 ministers who report to a Cabinet Secretary. Including the two law officers (Lord Advocate and Solicitor General for Scotland), this makes a total of 21 ministers.

Cabinet portfolios

The nine Cabinet Secretaries have responsibility for these nine areas:

- First Minister
- Finance, Employment and Sustainable Growth
- Health, Wellbeing and Cities Strategy
- Education and Lifelong Learning
- Justice
- Rural Affairs and Environment
- Culture and External Affairs
- Parliamentary Business and Government Strategy
- Infrastructure and Capital Investment

TOP TIP

Use this link to find out more about ministerial roles and responsibilities: www.gov.scot/About/People/Ministers

Relationship with Westminster

The Calman Commission published a report in 2009 that reviewed the provisions made under the Scotland Act 1998 and made recommendations to the constitutional arrangements that would enable the Scottish Parliament to better serve the people of Scotland. It outlined the areas where cooperation between Holyrood and Westminster were evident – law making, transfer of further powers such as transport, implementation of UK policy and the achievements of the Scottish Parliament in its first 10 years. However it was also evident that there were still areas of conflict and contention that needed to be addressed in respect of reserved matters, funding of the Scottish Parliament and issues such as the 'West Lothian question'. Between 2009 and 2015 certain issues have continued to cause

David Cameron and Alex Salmond when they were Prime Minister and First Minister, respectively

conflict, given the fact that the UK government was a Conservative–Liberal Democrat coalition while the SNP ruled in Scotland. The issue of independence and the subsequent referendum has undoubtedly led to increased conflict with regard to further transfer of powers and the negotiations that are underway around this. This has further been intensified given the number of SNP MPs currently at Westminster. The 56 SNP MPs currently at Westminster can certainly pose problems for the Cameron-led government, as was highlighted during the discussions on fox hunting.

Quick Test

1. Summarise the main role and powers of the First Minister.
2. Explain the term 'collective responsibility'.
3. Outline the areas where cooperation and conflict are evident between Holyrood and Westminster.

Electoral systems: First Past the Post (FPTP)

To ensure that you are confident in this section of the course you should be able to describe the different voting systems in use in the United Kingdom. You should also be able to evaluate each of the voting systems and the impact each has on election results. The simplest way to do this is to look at each system and its advantages and disadvantages relative to the others, using recent election results to support your knowledge and understanding.

First Past the Post (FPTP)

First Past the Post is used to elect representatives in many countries across the world. After Party List, it is the second most popular worldwide electoral system. It is used in the UK to elect members of the House of Commons, in the USA to elect members to Congress and in Canada and India to elect members of the lower houses.

FPTP is used in single member constituencies where the electorate simply mark a cross on the ballot paper next to their preferred candidate. The candidate with the most votes in each constituency wins. The simplistic nature of FPTP is often cited as being one of the key reasons for retaining it as the electoral system of choice in the UK, however there are continual calls for it to be replaced with a more proportionate system.

Advantages of FPTP

✓ It is simple to understand – voters mark a cross next to their preferred candidate and the candidate with the most votes wins. It is therefore simple to operate and count, and the result can be established very quickly. In 2015 Houghton and Sunderland South announced the winning candidate in the constituency only 50 minutes after the polls had closed. In some constituencies the winner has been declared within an hour of the polls closing. As a result, the electorate will usually have a clear idea by the next morning of which political party will form the next government.

✓ It provides a clear link between the representative and the constituents, ultimately giving more effective and accountable representation. Some MPs establish this relationship over a long period of time and remain as the representative for a number of years; Anne McGuire was the MP for Stirling from 1997 to 2015 for example.

✓ It usually produces a strong and stable government. Political parties usually have a majority of seats to exercise control over decision making and can implement their manifesto without the negotiation and compromise often caused by a coalition. It gives the political party the opportunity to deliver the policies they were committed to prior to being elected.

✓ It keeps extremism from entering mainstream politics. First Past the Post makes it far more difficult for smaller, radical parties to gain seats and therefore influence, for example UKIP polled 12.6% of the vote in 2015 yet only secured one seat.

Disadvantages of FPTP

✗ FPTP is often criticised for having a large number of 'wasted' votes: those cast for the losing candidates and those cast beyond the winning margin for the successful candidate.

✗ MPs can be elected with a tiny majority of votes. In Berwickshire, Roxburgh and Selkirk Calum Kerr SNP won the seat in 2015 with a majority of 328; Conservative MP Byron Davies has only a majority of 27 in the constituency of Gower. In marginal constituencies representatives can often find that more voters actually voted against them than for them. Critics would argue this is not democratic.

✗ The number of seats won by a party is not proportionate to the number of votes gained and it could therefore be argued that we do not get a fair result. In 2005 the Labour Party won the election with 35.2% of the vote yet secured 355 seats (55%). The Liberal Democrats, on the other hand, in 2010 managed to accrue 23% of the vote yet only won 8.7% of the seats.

TOP TIP

Follow the link www. voterpower.org.uk to see how much 'voter power' you have in your constituency.

✗ FPTP can lead to tactical voting as voters will often not vote for their preferred candidate if they don't think they have a chance of winning. They might instead vote for the candidate that they believe has the best chance of beating the candidate they most dislike.

General election results, 2015

Political party	% of vote	Number of MPs	% of seats	Seats gained/ lost from 2010
Conservative	36.9	331	50.9	+24
Labour	30.4	232	35.7	−26
Liberal Democrat	7.9	8	1.2	−49
SNP	4.7	56	8.6	+50
UKIP	12.6	1	0.15	+1

TOP TIP

Teach the teacher – as part of your revision in class ask your teacher if you could deliver a 10 minute revision session on First Past the Post. This will help not only you, but also the rest of the class.

Quick Test

1. Summarise the key advantages and disadvantages of First Past the Post.

2. Using the 2015 election results above, evaluate how fair the overall outcome of the general election was; consider the relative success of the parties in relation to the % of the vote gained.

Electoral systems: the Additional Member System (AMS)

The Additional Member System is a hybrid system that combines elements of both First Past the Post and the Party List. Each constituent is given two votes, one to elect an individual constituency representative and the other to vote for a specific party for a larger region of the country. The political parties will have already preselected a list of potential candidates for this area. In Scottish Parliament elections for example, constituents in Stirling will vote for an individual to represent them in the constituency and they will also select a party who they wish to represent them on the larger regional level of Mid Scotland and Fife, these are the Additional Members.

In the Scottish Parliament the constituency ballot is used to elect the 73 constituency members, with the second vote allowing constituents to elect the 56 regional members – seven from eight different regions, totalling 129 MSPs.

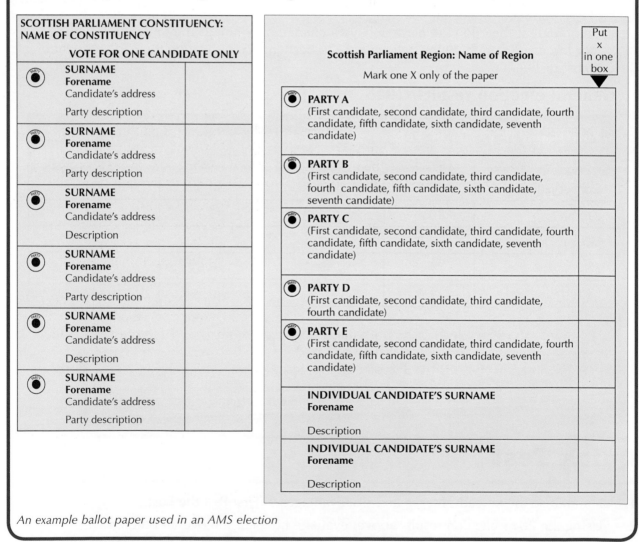

An example ballot paper used in an AMS election

Advantages of AMS

✓ It retains the accountability of constituency representation with the added bonus of proportionality through the additional members. The results should also be generally proportional with fewer votes being regarded as wasted.

✓ It gives smaller parties a chance of representation in the Scottish Parliament. Not all voters in Scotland support the large, established parties. The AMS has allowed success for the Greens, Scottish Socialist Party (SSP) and independents. The Green Party actively campaign on the second ballot rather than spend time fielding constituency candidates who are unlikely to win.

✓ AMS will usually produce coalition or minority government. The first three elections to the Scottish Parliament witnessed this – 1999 and 2003 saw a coalition formed between Labour and the Liberal Democrats and 2007 saw the SNP form a minority government. This promotes political debate, negotiation and compromise.

✓ It allows voters a greater choice. A voter can 'split their ticket' – supporting a candidate in the constituency vote from one party and using the regional ballot to vote for a different party or an independent candidate.

Disadvantages of AMS

✗ It appears to create two different kinds of representative – one for the constituency, who was elected as an individual and is directly accountable, and another who was elected under the guise of their party. The status of the additional members is often called into question as it has been suggested that they owe their seat more to the party placing them high on the list rather than being elected for their individual merits.

✗ By keeping an element of First Past the Post, true proportionality is not achieved.

✗ Parties become more powerful than voters. Political parties will exercise a great deal of control over the regional lists and potential candidates may well see party loyalty and support as the key to success rather than being truly supportive and accountable to constituents.

✗ AMS can often result in a government no-one voted for. The coalitions in the Scottish Parliament between 1999 and 2007 allowed the Liberal Democrats, who had actually came fourth in the election, to hold the balance of power. They were rewarded with senior positions in the Cabinet and many of their policies were implemented as a result of the compromise and debate. Furthermore many critics argued that Labour policies were compromised to gain support from the Liberal Democrats.

Scottish Parliament election results, 2011

Political party	Constituency MSPs	Regional MSPs	Total MSPs	% of votes	% of seats
Conservative	3	12	15	13.15	11.6
Green	0	2	2	2.2	1.6
Labour	15	22	37	29	28.7
Liberal Democrats	2	3	5	6.55	3.9
Scottish National Party	53	16	69	44.7	53.5
Independent (Margo MacDonald)	–	1	1	0.45	0.8
Others	0	0	0	3.95	–

TOP TIP

Use the Scottish Parliament website's education section at www.scottish.parliament.uk/visitandlearn/education.aspx to get the most up-to-date information and election results.

Quick Test

1. Summarise how the Additional Member System works in Scotland.
2. What makes AMS a more fair electoral system than FPTP? Use the election results to provide evidence to support your answer.

Electoral systems: Single Transferable Vote (STV)

STV is another form of proportional representation (PR) used in the UK – in Scotland STV is used in elections to local government, and in Northern Ireland it is used to elect local government, Members to the European Parliament and the Northern Ireland Assembly.

How STV works

In practice, representatives are elected from multi-member constituencies/wards. In Scotland constituents are voting to elect three or four council members to each local council ward. It is a system of preferential voting, so each constituent ranks the candidates in order of preference, meaning placing a '1' next to their most desired candidate, a '2' next to their second most desired and so on.

A quota of votes would be established, using what is known as the Droop quota:

$$Votes\ to\ win = \left(\frac{Valid\ votes\ cast}{Seats\ to\ be\ filled + 1}\right) + 1$$

If any candidate achieved this quota with first preference votes then he/she would automatically be elected. The surplus votes of the winners would be redistributed to those who did not reach the quota. If not enough candidates have reached the quota, the candidate with the lowest number of votes is eliminated and all of their votes are passed to the next preference on the ballot papers. This process repeats until either a winner is found for every seat or there are as many seats as remaining candidates. This ensures that a voter's preferences on the ballot paper determine how the votes are distributed. No votes appear to be wasted using this system.

Election for Aberdeen City Council
Bridge of Don Ward

Mark the figure '1' opposite the name of the candidate who is your first choice then mark the figure '2' opposite the name of the candidate who is your second choice and so on. You can mark as many choices as you wish but you must number them in order.
Do not mark your ballot paper with an 'X' or a '✔' or any other mark or symbol

INDEPENDENT	Canavan, Dennis 14c Love Lane, Linford, LN1 4PD	
INDEPENDENT	MacDonald, Margo 12 Grafton Grove, Bromham, AB12 3CD	
SCOTTISH CONSERVATIVE AND UNIONIST PARTY	Goldie, Annabel 55 Camellia Crescent, Linford, LN8 3DK	Scottish Conservatives
SCOTTISH CONSERVATIVE AND UNIONIST PARTY	McLetchie, David 94 Highland Grove, Bromham, AB18 9QR	Scottish Conservatives
SCOTTISH GREEN PARTY	Baird, Shiona 9 Heaven's Gate, Clifftop, LN18 4XS	
SCOTTISH LABOUR PARTY	Jamieson, Cathy 16 Thames Close, Bromham, AB13 4EF	Labour
SCOTTISH LABOUR PARTY	McConnell, Jack 24 Wallace Walk, Linford, LN4 9BY	Labour
SCOTTISH LABOUR PARTY	Peacock, Peter 6 South Africa Road, Horwood, N1 3FG	Labour
SCOTTISH LIBERAL DEMOCRATS	Stephen, Nicol 25 Trebor Road, Horwood, N1 9TV	
SCOTTISH LIBERAL DEMOCRATS	Wallace, Jim 6 South Road, Bigtown, KL1 3FG	
SCOTTISH NATIONAL PARTY	Lochhead, Richard 70 Rock Close, Bromham, AB21 12WX	
SCOTTISH NATIONAL PARTY	Sturgeon, Nicola 6 Sea Grove, Horwood, N1 6MN	
SCOTTISH NATIONAL PARTY	Swinney, John 6 Post Office Grove , Bigtown, KL1 6MN	
SCOTTISH SOCIALIST PARTY	Fox, Colin 386 Burns Drive, Linford, LN5 7RF	Scottish Socialist Party

An example ballot paper used in a STV election

Case study: Bannockburn Ward

These are the results for the local elections in Bannockburn Ward on 4 May, 2012.

Valid ballots	**3297**
Positions to be filled	**3**
Quota	**825**

Quota: $(3297 / (3+1)) + 1$

Stage 1 first preferences

Margaret Brisley	1133	Elected and surplus votes transferred (Stage 3)
David Kaufman	34	
Alasdair Macpherson	1236	Elected and surplus votes transferred (Stage 2)
Bill McDonald	165	
Gerard McLaughlan	187	
Lesley Stein	157	
Violet Weir	385	

It took another four stages before Violet Weir was elected.

TOP TIP

Look on the website of your own local authority and find the election results from 2012. The **transfer report** will help you understand the number of stages it took for your councillor to be elected. The link below will take you to the result for Stirling Council: www.stirling.gov.uk/services/council-and-government/politicians-elections-and-democracy/elections-and-voting/election-results/2012-local-elections

Advantages of STV

✓ Voters are able to rank candidates from within the same party, which allows voters to judge the candidates on their beliefs, opinions and past voting records. Due to its preferential nature the system also allows voters to vote across parties, perhaps for an independent candidate who is campaigning on a single issue about which they feel strongly. In 2012 independent candidates polled over 183,000 first preference votes, which was more than was polled for Liberal Democrat candidates.

✓ Due to the surplus votes being redistributed, voters feel like all votes count and none are wasted, giving a highly proportionate result. In 2012 the SNP achieved 32.33% of the first preference votes and accumulated 425 seats (34%), with Labour achieving 394 seats (32%) with 31.39% of the first preference votes.

✓ Voters have a choice of representatives to whom they can take their issues. Within the Hillhead Ward of Glasgow City Council, each voter has a choice of four representatives, representing three different parties: SNP, Labour and Green.

Disadvantages of STV

✗ Multi-member constituencies are often criticised for weakening the positive link formed between individual MPs and constituents under FPTP.

✗ The degree of proportionality for less popular parties is often criticised. In 2012 the Conservatives secured 13.27% of the first preference votes but only gained 115 seats, which is just over 9%.

✗ Coalition governments are likely to occur. The results in Scotland after 2012 left 23 local authorities with no single party in overall control. Labour secured control over only four councils, SNP gained control of two councils and independents retained control of the Western Isles, Shetland and Orkney.

Quick Test

1. Summarise the key advantages and disadvantages of Single Transferable Vote.
2. What feature of STV gives it a high level of proportionality?
3. What difficulties might local authorities face if there is no single party with overall control? You could try to find an example of where this has been a problem to support your answer.

Electoral systems: Party List

Party List is a further form of PR, which is used in Israel and countries throughout Europe. It is currently used in Scotland, England and Wales to elect members to the European Parliament (as well as being the format for electing the Additional Members to the Scottish Parliament).

How MEPs are elected

The UK is divided into 12 electoral regions, each electing a number of MEPs (between three and 10). In total the UK has 73 MEPs representing us in the European Parliament.

The UK uses a 'closed list' where voters simply vote for a party rather than an individual. Parties select the candidates list themselves and are allocated seats in proportion to the number of votes they achieve, using a mathematical method called the D'Hondt formula. Candidates at the top of each party list are more likely to be elected than those further down.

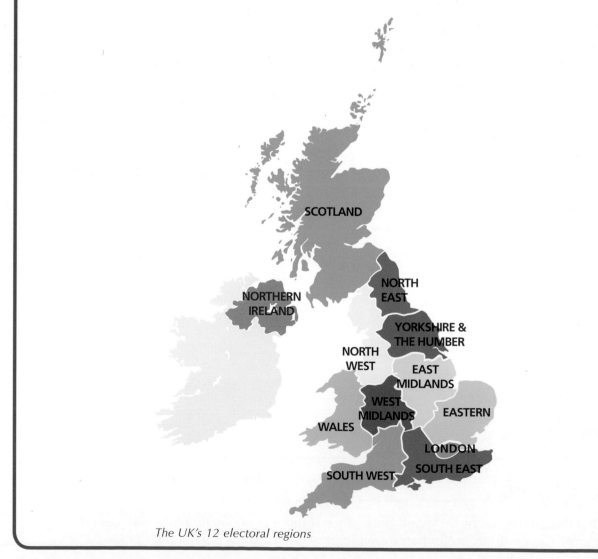

The UK's 12 electoral regions

Advantages of Party List

✓ Voting could not be simpler – each voter has one vote for either one party or an independent candidate.

✓ A higher degree of proportionality is guaranteed than when using FPTP, although it may not appear completely proportional. In 2014 UKIP acquired 27.49% of the vote across the UK and won 24 seats (17%), with Labour gaining 25.4% of the vote and gaining 20 seats (14.6%).

✓ Closed lists make it easier for women and ethnic minorities to be elected. In 2014, 41% of MEPs elected in the UK were women.

Disadvantages of Party List

✗ As a result of proportionality, many smaller parties and sometimes more extreme parties can gain power. This could lead to instability. In the 2014 European Parliament election, UKIP came top in the election in the UK. Previous to this, the BNP had won two seats in the 2009 election (they lost both in 2014).

✗ The close link between constituents and representatives formed under FPTP does not exist. People in Scotland have a choice of only six MEP representatives in total.

✗ As with the AMS, political parties become more powerful than voters. Any party member who is likely to deviate from the party line will be unlikely to feature high on the list.

TOP TIP

Try this survey in your class: how many of your classmates can name the six MEPs who represent Scotland?

Quick Test

1. Identify the key features of the Party List electoral system.
2. Summarise the main advantages and disadvantages.

Voting behaviour: social class

Psephologists (political scientists who study elections) continue to analyse how individuals in society interact with politics. They do this in the hope that they will be able to draw conclusions about the nature of voting patterns and political parties would, therefore, be able to predict where to target their campaigning. However over the years it has become evident that voting behaviour is shaped by both short- and long-term influences and it is often difficult to make conclusions about overall patterns of voting behaviour. We do know however that there are key factors that influence voting behaviour.

Social class and the electorate

Analysis of voting behaviour began in 1945 using an individual's socio-economic status. At this time groups A, B and C1 were traditionally Conservative supporters while social classes C2, D and E voted Labour. This was mainly due the political parties' ideas meeting the needs of each of the groups, e.g. Conservatives believed in limited government interference while Labour championed the redistribution of wealth. Over time class has appeared to be less influential and the idea of **class dealignment** grew in importance. There is clear evidence of this in more recent elections, see the table below.

	Class AB voters	Class C1 voters	Class C2 voters	Class DE voters
2001				
Conservative	39%	36%	29%	24%
Labour	30%	38%	49%	55%
2005				
Conservative	37%	37%	33%	25%
Labour	28%	32%	40%	48%
2010				
Conservative	39%	39%	37%	31%
Labour	26%	28%	29%	40%
2015				
Conservative	45%	41%	32%	27%
Labour	26%	29%	32%	41%

Source: Ipsos MORI

It could be argued that this continued shift in voting behaviour occurs as a result of political parties adopting a more 'catch-all' approach to their policies, in order to attract the highest number of voters. However we have to consider other factors that might impact on how citizens vote.

Over time class has appeared to be less influential on voting behaviour

TOP TIP

Use the following link to gain further information relating to factors that affected voting behaviour in 2015: www.ipsos-mori.com/researchpublications/researcharchive/3575/How-Britain-voted-in-2015

Quick Test

1. Why do psephologists continue to analyse voting patterns in the UK?
2. Using the results table, analyse the changes that have occurred with regard to voting and social class between 2001 and 2010.
3. Using the internet, compare the policies of the three main political parties in the 2015 general election and identify three policies that could be described as 'catch-all'.

Voting behaviour: geographical location

Does where you live influence how you vote?

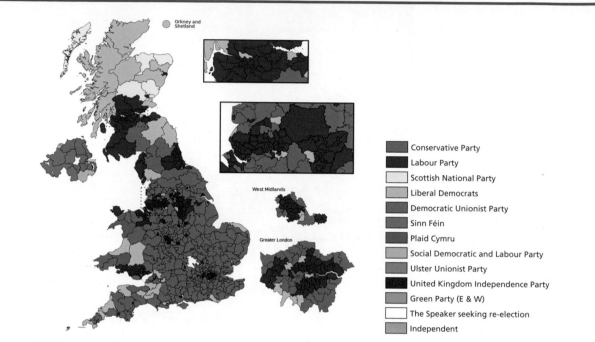

Orkney and Shetland

West Midlands

Greater London

Conservative Party
Labour Party
Scottish National Party
Liberal Democrats
Democratic Unionist Party
Sinn Féin
Plaid Cymru
Social Democratic and Labour Party
Ulster Unionist Party
United Kingdom Independence Party
Green Party (E & W)
The Speaker seeking re-election
Independent

2010 general election results map

This question has been a major focus in recent years due to the continued 'North/South divide'. From the map it is evident that in 2010 the majority of the support for the Conservative party lay in the south of the UK as well as suburban and rural areas, with support for Labour occurring in the north of England, Scotland and parts of Wales, mainly in urban areas and large cities. This can also be linked to social class, as large numbers of social class C2, D and E are often concentrated in urban areas.

Political parties pay great attention to regional support as due to the way FPTP voting works they can often focus their election campaigns in specific areas, hoping to win a number of marginal constituencies. In 2010 it was evident that close-fought contests occurred between Labour and the Conservatives in London, the Midlands, the Northwest and Yorkshire, while the main battlegrounds in the Southwest were fought between the Conservatives and Liberal Democrats. In Scotland and Wales the nationalist parties – SNP and Plaid Cymru – were often beaten into second place.

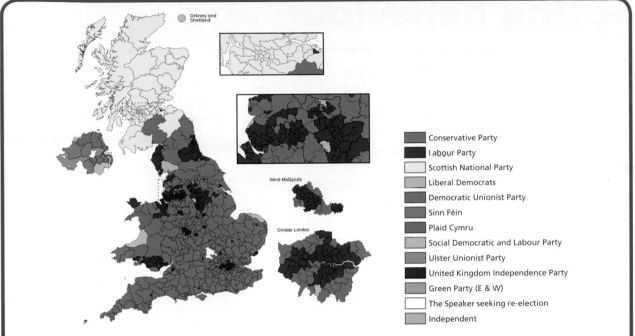

2015 general election results map

However in 2015 parties identified key target seats. The constituency of Dorset Mid and Poole North had a Liberal Democrat majority of only 269 and became a key target for the Conservatives given that they had wide support in the surrounding areas. This was to be successful in that the Conservatives took the seat with a 10,530 majority. In the Edinburgh South constituency, Labour had a majority of only 316 which made it a key target, however it was to be the only seat they managed to retain. Elsewhere in Scotland the SNP won 56 of the 59 seats available.

> **TOP TIP**
>
> Use the following link to gain further information on voting patterns across the UK: www.earlhamsociologypages.co.uk/vbint.htm

Quick Test

1. Explain what you understand by the 'North/South divide'.

2. Why do political parties pay an interest in regional support during elections?

3. Thurrock was the most marginal seat in the UK in 2015 with a Conservative majority of 92. Which political parties do you think targeted this seat? Explain why. You may have to do some online research to answer this question.

Voting behaviour: age

Age and voting behaviour

Age appears to be a significant influence on voting behaviour and can have an impact on elections. Various explanations have been given for this, such as different age groups having different life experiences – the older the voter the more loyal they may be to a particular party (in the period 1992–2015, the over 50s in general favoured the Conservatives). Younger voters, on the other hand, are less likely to vote overall, with only 43% of 18–24 year-olds voting in 2015. This is also supported by the fact that Conservatives managed to gain voters in the 65+ age group, which is the group with the highest turnout (78%), whereas Labour do well with the 18–24 age group, whose turnout is lowest.

TOP TIP

Read the following article for more information on the importance of age: www.theguardian.com/politics/2015/may/22/election-2015-who-voted-for-whom-labour-conservatives-turnout

Age and the 2015 general election

The table below highlights how the UK voted by age in 2015.

	Con %	Lab %	LD %	UKIP %	Green	Other	Con lead over Lab ± %	Turnout %	Con ± %	Lab ± %	LD ± %	Turnout ± %	Con-Lab swing %
18–24	27	43	5	8	8	9	–16	43	–3	+12	–25	–1	7.5
25–34	33	36	7	10	7	7	–3	54	–2	+6	–22	–1	4
35–44	35	35	10	10	4	6	0	64	+1	+4	–16	–2	1.5
45–54	36	33	8	14	4	5	3	72	+2	+5	–18	+3	1.5
55–64	37	31	9	14	2	7	6	77	–1	+3	–14	+4	2
65+	47	23	8	17	2	3	24	78	+3	–8	–8	+2	–5.5

Source: Ipsos MORI

What is evident is that the Labour party made gains in all age groups apart from 65+, with a major gain in 18–24. This appeared to be at the expense of the Liberal Democrats who lost voters in all age groups. It appears that the older voters were more likely to switch to Conservative or UKIP.

Age and the 2014 referendum

In 2014 younger voters played a key role in the referendum because 16 and 17-year-olds were entitled to vote. More than 109,000 younger voters were registered to vote, apparently voting in favour of independence. The Lord Ashcroft Poll suggested that 71% of 16–17-years-olds voted Yes with 29% voting No (however the poll had a very small sample size). However YouGov's final poll of 3188 voters showed that 51 per cent of those aged between 16 and 24 voted No.

Should we link age to other factors such as issue voting? MORI polls would suggest that at times issues can play a more important role for younger voters than the party leader or party policies. In the 2014 referendum the key issues affecting voting appeared to be the NHS, currency, defence and the EU. In the 2015 general election the main issues influencing voting behaviour were the economy, immigration, NHS/health, education and benefits. However, issues change over time and are regarded as short-term influences that are often a reflection of the political climate.

Younger voters played a key role in the referendum

Quick Test

1. What evidence is there that older votes continually support the same political party?

2. Why are issues regarded as short-term influences in relation to voting behaviour?

Voting behaviour: gender

Before 1997 women were more likely to vote Conservative than men, however the landslide Labour victory of 1997, the increase in the number of women in parliament and the further victory for Labour in 2001 could all be attributed to the shift in the voting habits of women. During the late 1990s and early 2000s both men and women appeared to favour Labour. However, by 2010 gender voting patterns had shifted once again. Political parties began to target women on the basis that they could swing the vote and ultimately win a party an election. Political leaders opted for campaign tactics that they assumed would be influential in gaining the female vote. Politicians campaigned online via parenting websites such as Mumsnet and Netmums, which have a combined membership of almost 700,000.

2005 general election

It proved difficult to analyse gender voting patterns in 2005 as different polling organisations provided different results. The British Election Study (BES) indicated that 38% of men and 37% of women voted Labour and 31% of men and 34% of women voted Conservative, however MORI reported that 34% of men and 38% of women voted Labour compared to 34% of men and 32% of women who voted Conservative. Whichever results we look at we can suggest that women made a contribution to the Labour win.

David Cameron courting the female vote

2015 general election

These figures show the percentage by gender of voters in the 2015 general election:

	Conservative	Labour	Liberal Democrat
Male	38	30	8
Female	37	33	8

Source: Ipsos MORI

These results highlight a loss in support for the Liberal Democrats from both men and women, with Conservatives and Labour making gains. This may have been the result of the clear manifesto attempts to attract women, especially those who may have been undecided. Shortly after becoming leader of the Conservatives David Cameron highlighted that key priorities for him were reducing gender inequalities and improving childcare. More recently we have witnessed all-women shortlists in elections and a number of political movements developing, such as 'Women for Independence', highlighting the continued interest in gender-specific politics. This will continue to keep politicians interested in courting the female vote in forthcoming elections.

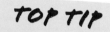

TOP TIP

Pay attention to the manifestos published prior to the Scottish Parliament election in 2016 – you will be able to identify policies that are aimed at gaining the female vote.

The Liberal Democrats lost support from both men and women in the 2015 general election

Quick Test

1. What evidence is there to highlight a shift in the voting patterns of women after 1997?
2. Why would politicians such as David Cameron view it as beneficial to gain support from online forums such as Mumsnet and Netmums?

Voting behaviour: ethnicity

Evidence suggests that ethnic minority voters are far less likely to vote than white voters – this is attributed to a number of reasons.

Labour and ethnic minorities

Encouraging ethnic minorities to vote has been a problem for a number of years. People from ethnic minority groups often believe that their vote will make little difference. This has been partially due to the high concentrations of ethnic minorities in safe Labour seats, where poverty and deprivation are common. In the past the ethnic minority vote has typically gone to Labour. Ethnic minorities are still more likely to vote Labour than the rest of the population, however over time the support for Labour has decreased, with support for the Conservatives recently increasing.

Conservatives and ethnic minorities

Political parties have come to realise the importance of the ethnic minority vote and have made concerted efforts to appear to be 'all inclusive' parties. David Cameron has tried to ensure that the Conservatives are not seen as anti-immigration in order to avoid conflict with, and lack of support from, ethnic minorities. This may have been somewhat successful given that a third of voters (over one million people) from ethnic minorities voted Conservative in the 2015 election – the first time this has happened. Although Labour remained well ahead, gaining 52% of ethnic minority votes, the gap between the two parties seems to be shrinking. A survey conducted by Survation in the days after the election revealed interesting differences in party support by ethnic groups, showing much greater support for the Conservatives among Asian voters:

- Asian: 50% Labour, 38% Conservative
- Black: 67% Labour, 21% Conservative
- Mixed race: 49% Labour, 26% Conservative

Ethnic minority candidates

In the 2015 general election there were still limited opportunities to vote for ethnic minority candidates – of the 650 constituencies in the UK, ethnic minority candidates only stood in 167. However, although ethnic minorities are still under-represented in the House of Commons, the situation has been improving: the 2015 election also saw the number of ethnic minority MPs rise to 37 – the highest number ever, with Alan Mak becoming the first MP of Chinese origin. This is a rise from 15 MPs in 2005 and 27 in 2010.

Quick Test

1. List three reasons why ethnic minorities are less likely to vote than white people.
2. What have political parties done to encourage ethnic minorities to vote for them?
3. What evidence is there that ethnic minorities may have been influential in 2015?

The impact of the mass media on voting behaviour: television

There is great debate as to how influential the media can be. On the one hand it could be argued that the mass media simply reflect as well as reinforce political preferences that are already established. However it could be argued that the mass media are able to distort the flow of political information by setting the agenda for debate and transmitting information when and how they see fit, easily manipulating the voting intentions of the undecided.

Television as mass media

For the majority of the population TV is still the most widely used form of media: in October 2013 an Ofcom survey found that UK households spent an average of four hours per day watching TV, compared to 1.15 hours using the internet; it follows that most people's main source of political information is television news broadcasts and current affairs programmes. In the days prior to any election there is extensive TV coverage of the campaign and this has huge potential to shape political attitudes, given that TV is still the favoured and trusted source of information for the majority of the population. This may be due to the fact that TV is regulated (TV coverage should be impartial) however all political parties have complained about the BBC at some point. Politicians and political parties use TV to promote a positive image, with sound bites being carefully planned and speeches reduced to concise statements to be more easily quotable.

Gordon Brown was picked up by a TV microphone referring to a member of the public as a 'bigoted woman' in 2010, throwing his campaign into turmoil

The rise of the TV debate

In 2010 TV debates were held between the three main party leaders, with 9.9 million viewers tuning in to the first debate. In this first debate it was Liberal Democrat leader Nick Clegg who emerged the overall winner. The first substantial poll, conducted by Populus, for *The Times* found Clegg the overwhelming winner with 61% and Cameron and Brown trailing on 22% and 17% respectively. This debate was replicated in 2014 prior to the referendum with Alex Salmond and Alistair Darling going head-to-head, with an estimated 843,000 viewers. Further debates were broadcast from around Scotland in the weeks prior to the actual vote. But how influential was TV?

In 2010 the Liberal Democrat vote went up 1% overall in the UK, however they lost five seats, so it could be argued that the debates and the popularity of Clegg made no difference. David Cameron and the Conservatives managed to maintain a positive image – TV helped perhaps and they increased their share of the vote by 3.8%, gaining 97 seats. Labour lost 91 seats and decreased their share of the vote by 6.2%. Could we argue therefore that this was a combination of TV influence and a poor image of the party leader?

In 2015 more than a third of voters were said to have been influenced by the TV debates. A Panelbase survey found 38% were influenced by the debates, 23% by TV news coverage and 10% by party political broadcasts. In April 2015 an average audience of 7 million viewers watched the leaders debate on ITV, the only live debate in which David Cameron took part. The survey further highlighted the power of TV with only 25% stating newspapers had been influential in helping form their opinions compared with the 62% who stated TV as being most influential. Websites at 17% and radio at 14% proved insignificant in comparison.

In Scotland the BBC were criticised prior to the 2014 referendum by 'Yes Scotland' supporters on a number of occasions for demonstrating political bias towards the 'No' campaign as well as not giving enough air time to the issue.

Quick Test

1. Why is TV still regarded as influential in shaping voting behaviour?
2. What has been the most significant change in TV political coverage since 2010?
3. Based on the 2010 election result could we argue that TV was influential to a certain extent? Give evidence to support your answer.

The impact of the mass media on voting behaviour: newspapers

Newspapers can have great influence, given that they play an important role in providing political information. Newspapers are not neutral, they decide which stories are covered and how they are covered, and are often clearly in favour of one party or another and are inclined to switch support over time. As a result they are in a powerful position to influence public opinion and will often take credit for securing victory for a party.

Newspapers' political allegiances

In 1997 the *Sun* famously backed Tony Blair and the Labour Party, the predicted winners of that year's election. However by September 2009 they ran a front page headline stating 'Labour's Lost It', highlighting the end of their support for the Labour Party. Following on from that, in 2010 they printed a front page in the style of the 2008 US Obama campaign, showing support for David Cameron and the Conservatives – significantly by this point the Conservatives were already ahead in the opinion polls.

When considering newspaper readership and voting patterns there is evidence that suggests influence. Fifty-nine per cent of those reading the *Daily Mirror* in 2010, a clear supporter of Labour, voted Labour, with 70% of *Telegraph* readers voting Conservative. However we have to consider again whether this could be a simple reinforcement of pre-existing opinions.

In 2007 the *Scottish Sun* supported the Labour party in the run-up to the 2007 Scottish Parliament election, yet the SNP won the largest number of MSPs and formed a minority government. By 2011 the *Scottish Sun* supported the SNP and their share of MSPs increased significantly, allowing them to form a majority government.

In recent years there has been growing concern about the influence that the press can exert over political parties. It is argued that political parties have actively courted the press, showing their recognition of its influence. However, there is a danger that the ownership of the media is concentrated in too few hands and as a result they

The Sun's *2010 cover*

The Scottish Sun's *opinion of the SNP has changed since 2007*

are able to shape public opinion and influence voting behaviour. This was further evident in 2015 when the *Scottish Sun* supported the SNP yet in the rest of the UK the *Sun* supported the Conservatives. The lack of impartiality may lead to a loss of trust among readers.

The Scottish Sun *side-by-side with its UK equivalent*

Quick Test

1. What is the key difference between newspapers and TV with regard to political coverage?
2. What evidence is there that newspapers can have an impact on their readers' voting behaviour?
3. What evidence is there that newspapers have limited impact on voting behaviour?

The impact of the mass media on voting behaviour: internet and social media

In recent years we have witnessed an immense growth in the use of the internet and social media by both political parties and politicians in an attempt to influence voting behaviour. The web acts as a key source of information and a valuable method of communication for all involved. Political party websites, political blogs and forums, 24-hour news online, YouTube and social media networking sites such as Facebook and Twitter have been actively used in order to engage the general population in politics.

Facebook and Twitter as political tools

In the run-up to the 2010 general election Downing Street and Sarah Brown (wife of Labour leader Gordon Brown) had over one million followers on Twitter and more than 100 MPs were reported as using Twitter to communicate with the electorate. As a result the 2010 general election was hailed by the *Guardian* as the first social media election. Research highlighted that Facebook's 'Democracy UK' page engaged many voters in the election process by allowing them to debate the issues in their own space; this is backed up by the over 270,000 'likes' it received and that almost a million votes were cast in their poll. Facebook also partnered with the Electoral Commission on a voter registration page through which 14,000 registration forms were downloaded, showing how seriously the establishment now takes the influence of social media. Facebook also developed an app to be used in conjunction with the televised debates – 'rate the debate' and it became commonplace for many voters to 'double gaze' – that is, watch the debate on TV whilst commenting on social media.

Smartphones make it easy to access political information online

In September 2015 Tweetminster reported that over 430 MPs were using Twitter. David Cameron and the UK government have their own YouTube channel (www.youtube.com/user/Number10gov) where 'exclusive films and features from Downing Street and the Prime Minister' are posted.

Social media and the referendum

In the run-up to the independence referendum the internet and social media were key political campaign tools. Both 'Yes Scotland' and 'Better Together' used the internet widely to campaign. Researchers from the University of Glasgow mapped the use of '#indyref' to see how each side used social media in their campaign, and released a monthly snapshot. The BBC debate held in the SSE Hydro for 16- and 17-year-olds encouraged them to comment on Twitter using '#bigbigdebate', engaging a generation in political activity through the media they most widely use.

The Internet and social media were used heavily in the independence referendum

Social media and the 2015 general election

However, Rory Cellan-Jones (BBC Technology Correspondent) suggested that in 2015 social media 'followed the campaign rather than led it'. Although campaigners as well as politicians used social media extensively, Cellan-Jones stated that the newspapers made the running, concluding, 'it wasn't social media "wot won it"'.

TOP TIP
You can read Cellan-Jones' full article here: www.bbc.co.uk/news/technology-32689145

Quick Test

1. List the different online measures used to engage the general population in politics.

2. Has the use of social media changed over the years? Give evidence to support your answer.

3. Which group may be the most influenced by social media when making a political decision? Explain why.

Participation

How do citizens participate in the UK?

UK citizens are able to participate in a number of different ways. For the majority of UK citizens **voting** will be their main form of participation. Citizens are able to vote in a number of different elections:

- UK general election
- Regional elections to the Scottish Parliament, Welsh Assembly and the Northern Ireland Assembly
- Local government elections
- European Parliament elections
- Referenda
- By-elections

Turnout at these different elections is variable, highlighting that citizens are not consistent in their levels of participation.

Turnout rates

Turnout at these recent elections has been variable:

- UK general election 2015   66.1%
- Scottish Parliament election 2011   50.4%
- European Parliament election 2014   34.18% (EU average = 43.09%)
- Scottish independence referendum 2014   84.5%

In some areas of the UK citizens may also be able to participate in more specific elections such as those to elect the London Mayor or the London Assembly. However there are a huge number of opportunities for participation in addition to voting.

Methods of participation

Some methods of participation include:

- Standing as a candidate.
- Joining a political party.
- Becoming a member of a pressure group.
- Supporting a political campaign (e.g. canvassing on behalf of a candidate, leafleting, phone bank).
- Submitting an e-petition.

Case study: e-petitions (https://petition.parliament.uk)

Online petitions, or e-petitions, are a straightforward way of allowing UK citizens to influence government decision making. Citizens can submit an e-petition on anything for which the UK government is responsible. If the e-petition acquires at least 100,000 signatures it will be considered by the backbench Business Committee for a debate in the House of Commons. On a number of occasions e-petitions have gone as far as being debated on the floor of the House of Commons, for example the e-petition for the full disclosure of all government documents relating to the 1989 Hillsborough disaster. Recently the e-petition titled 'Sophie's Choice', campaigning to lower the age of cervical smear tests to 16, acquired 323,986 signatures.

TOP TIP

Visit the Scottish Parliament website at www.scottish.parliament.uk to find out the types of petitions being submitted in Scotland.

Quick Test

1. For the majority of UK citizens, what is their main form of participation?

2. Could citizens participate more in elections? Give evidence to support your answer.

3. Research a further e-petition and assess whether it had any impact or influence on government decision making.

Pressure groups

Pressure groups (interest groups) are groups of like-minded people who have come together as a result of their similar values and opinions. It is their intention to either bring about change or prevent change occurring and by joining or supporting a pressure group citizens aim to influence the political decision making process, on either a local, national or international level. There is a huge range in the size, type and variety of pressure groups, with some having been established for a lengthy period of time and others existing only until the change they are campaigning for has occurred.

Rights and responsibilities of pressure groups

Pressure groups have certain rights and responsibilities when attempting to influence the decision making process. They are free to inform the general public of their values and opinions and are able to campaign using a significant number of methods. However, alongside this pressure groups should also maintain high levels of respect for other citizens and organisations and ensure that their campaign methods remain legal.

The following rights and freedoms are protected in the UK by the Human Rights Act:

- Right to peaceful protest/freedom of assembly.
- Freedom of expression.
- Right to publicly criticise the government.

In addition pressure groups have the following responsibilities:

- Information given to the public must be accurate and not damage a person's or organisation's reputation.
- Protests should be carried out in a peaceful, legal manner.
- Pressure groups should not slander anyone or any organisation – this breaks defamation laws and the pressure group may be sued.

Methods used by pressure groups

Pressure groups attempt to attract attention to their cause by gaining widespread media publicity. Different pressure groups use different methods, ranging from simple petitions to more extreme publicity stunts. In 2009 members of Greenpeace were arrested for scaling Mount Rushmore and draping a banner to protest against global warming, just as the G8 Summit was about to begin in Italy.

The Greenpeace banner at Mount Rushmore

Other methods used by pressure groups may include:

- Demonstrations
- Publicity campaigns (leaflets, posters, online advertisements)
- Lobbying MPs/MSPs/councillors
- Mass/social media campaigns
- Public meetings
- Hiring professional lobbyists

Characteristics of different pressure groups

Insider (e.g. BMA, Age UK)	Outsider (e.g. Greenpeace, Fans Against Criminalisation)	Cause (e.g. RSPCA, PETA)	Interest (e.g. National Union of Journalists)
• High profile • Regarded by government as legitimate • Strong links with decision makers • Regularly consulted • Long-term political influence	• Work outside of government • Fewer opportunities to influence directly • Adopt different strategy to insider groups • Can be radical • Can be ideologically opposed to political system	• Promotes particular cause or value • Not self-interested • No formal restrictions on membership • Can rely on member donations	• Promotes particular interests • Aims to benefit its own members • Membership from particular sector • Fee paying

Case studies: pressure group success stories

Scothedge

After 14 years of campaigning, Scothedge, 'representing Scotland's unprotected high hedge and other nuisance vegetation victims', were successful in bringing about The High Hedges (Scotland) Act 2013, which came into force in April 2014. The Act aimed to solve the issue of high hedges, where neighbours had not been able to resolve the issue amicably, see www.scothedge.co.uk

Greenpeace

In 2014 Greenpeace achieved high levels of success in their campaign for hazardous chemicals to be removed from fashion clothing. High street retailers such as Primark along with international fashion houses such as Burberry and Valentino have agreed to eliminate these by 2020. Use the link to gain further information on the achievements of Greenpeace: www.greenpeace.org/international/en/about/victories

TOP TIP

Ensure that you are familiar with the aims of at least one local, national and international pressure group, focusing on their key successes and the methods they use to exert influence.

Quick Test

1. Outline what a pressure group is trying to achieve. Use the case studies to support your answer.

2. Do the methods that some pressure groups use go against their democratic rights and responsibilities? Give evidence to support your answer.

3. Based on the table of characteristics of pressure groups on page 78, which group would the following belong to? You may have to conduct some online research to help you decide:

   - British Medical Association
   - Fire Brigade Union
   - Greenpeace
   - Stirling Before Pylons
   - Child Poverty Action Group
   - Oxfam
   - Fathers for Justice (F4J)
   - National Farmers Union
   - CND

What is inequality?

> *'Difference in size, degree, circumstance, lack of equality.'*
>
> The Oxford Dictionary definition of inequality

Inequalities in income and health

The definition given above highlights that inequality relates to a **difference** in size and circumstance. In the UK when referring to inequality we can easily identify this difference with regard to the **wealth** and **health** of UK citizens.

Income inequalities have been increasing over a number of years with the poorest 10% of the population seeing a decrease in their incomes. Alongside this the richest 10% of the population have seen significant rises in their income. The *Guardian* newspaper reported in March 2014 that Britain's five richest families were worth more than the poorest 20% of the population. Based on the Oxfam report 'A Tale of Two Britains' it is estimated that the poorest 20% in the UK had wealth totalling £28.1 billion whilst the Forbes rich list's top five UK entries had property, savings and assets worth £28.2 billion.

Wealth is often held by the select few

Alongside income inequality the poorest in the UK appear to suffer the poorest health. The Kings Fund think tank (2012) found that England's richest citizens were likely to live seven years longer, on average, than those less well off. Although the survey found a reduction in the total number of people engaging in 'risky behaviours' – smoking, excess alcohol use, poor diet and a sedentary lifestyle – the type of people who were stopping smoking or drinking less were mainly in the higher socio-economic and educational groups. Further health inequalities are evident in Scotland, where a Scottish Government report highlighted that men and women in the most deprived communities can expect to spend 22.7 and 26.1 years respectively in 'not good health'. These examples are clear indicators that inequality exists in the UK.

Quick Test

1. What two key indicators can be used to assess inequality?
2. What evidence is there that the rich are getting richer and the poor are getting poorer?
3. What are the 'risky behaviours' that will undoubtedly impact on your health?

Evidence of inequalities in the UK

Poverty

Poverty is a key indicator that inequalities exist in the UK. Poverty can be measured in a number of ways; Peter Townsend, a sociologist and one of the founders of the Child Poverty Action Group, defined poverty as 'when they [families/individuals] lack resources to obtain the type of diet, participate in the activities and have the living conditions and amenities which are customary, or at least widely encouraged and approved, in the societies in which they belong'.

Poverty can be measured in a number of ways

However, the official government measure of poverty is households that earn 60% or less of median household income (Households Below Average Income, HBAI). In 2011–12 the amount of earnings before a household was said to be in poverty was £128 a week for a single adult; £172 for a single parent with one child; £220 for a couple with no children; and £357 for a couple with two children. The Joseph Rowntree Foundation (JRF) found that as a result more working households were living in poverty than those from workless households. The JRFs 'Monitoring Poverty and Social Exclusion Report' found that half of the 13 million people in poverty were actually from working families. They attributed this mainly to low pay and part-time work.

Socio-economic status

Recent evidence would suggest that there is a widening gap in wealth inequalities between those in the higher occupational classes and those in the lower occupational classes. In October 2014 a report was published highlighting the fact that Britain is the only country in the leading G7 economies where inequalities have become worse this century, with the richest 10% controlling 54.1% of the wealth, up from 51.5% in 2000. Charities such as Oxfam have suggested that these figures show 'more evidence that inequality is extreme and growing, and that economic recovery following the financial crisis has been skewed in favour of the wealthiest'. Furthermore, The Equality Trust indicated that income inequality in the UK had grown at an alarming rate – highlighting a vast difference between the average income of the richest, and the rest of the UK.

TOP TIP

You can look at the Equality Trust's findings in detail here: www.equalitytrust.org.uk/sites/default/files/Income%20Inequality%20UK.pdf

The BBC conducted a major survey entitled 'The Great British Class Survey' that suggested people in the UK now fit into seven categories, using measures of not just economic and social capital but also cultural capital. The seven categories identified were:

1. Elite

2. Established middle class

3. Technical middle class

4. New affluent workers

5. Traditional working class

6. Emergent service workers

7. Precariat, or precarious proletariat

TOP TIP

For further information on the Great British Class Survey visit: www.bbc.co.uk/news/uk-22007058

This further highlighted inequalities between different groups in society when considering earnings, occupation, education, housing tenure, social interactions and geographical location.

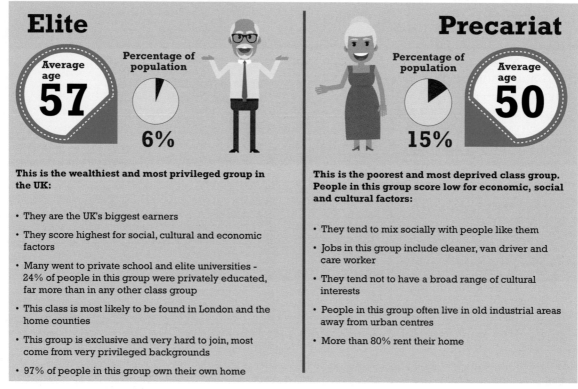

Elite

Average age

57

Percentage of population

6%

This is the wealthiest and most privileged group in the UK:

• They are the UK's biggest earners

• They score highest for social, cultural and economic factors

• Many went to private school and elite universities - 24% of people in this group were privately educated, far more than in any other class group

• This class is most likely to be found in London and the home counties

• This group is exclusive and very hard to join, most come from very privileged backgrounds

• 97% of people in this group own their own home

Precariat

Percentage of population

15%

Average age

50

This is the poorest and most deprived class group. People in this group score low for economic, social and cultural factors:

• They tend to mix socially with people like them

• Jobs in this group include cleaner, van driver and care worker

• They tend not to have a broad range of cultural interests

• People in this group often live in old industrial areas away from urban centres

• More than 80% rent their home

The Great British Class Survey

Data published in 2014 by the Treasury highlighted that the top 10% of earners in Britain have salaries that are equal to more than the bottom 40% of earners combined. Oxfam have also highlighted that Britain's five richest families are worth more than the poorest 20% of the country.

Further evidence to highlight the major wealth inequalities in the UK is the continued growth in the number of billionaires in the UK alongside the continuing high levels of poverty. The *Sunday Times* 'Rich List' for the UK in 2014 listed over 100 billionaires, with a combined wealth of over $507 billion – the largest number of billionaires proportionate to the population worldwide. London has more billionaires than any other city in the world, while also suffering huge levels of poverty. According to 'London's Poverty Profile', 28% of people are living in poverty, which is 7% higher than the rest of England. The profile also states that there is greater unemployment in London compared to the English average, as well as a quarter of people relying on housing benefit compared to a fifth across the rest of England. What does become evident is that factors causing inequalities are often inter-related, i.e. the lower your socio-economic status the more likely it is that you will be in poverty. This is further supported in the next section when looking at geographical inequalities.

Geographical inequalities

Inequalities and poverty levels vary across the UK, with poverty appearing more prevalent in the north than the south and in urban rather than rural areas. It is often a reflection of the lack of jobs and opportunities within certain areas and is therefore closely related to socio-economic status. The constituency profiles listed in the table below show that there are specific areas of the country that suffer more than others. The London borough of Tower Hamlets, home to the Bethnal Green and Bow constituency and the Poplar and Limehouse constituency, is one of the UK's most deprived areas, with one in two children in Tower Hamlets being raised in poor conditions.

Child poverty rates by constituency

	Constituency	% of children in poverty 2013 (after housing costs)
1.	Bethnal Green and Bow	49%
2.	Poplar and Limehouse	49%
3.	Birmingham, Ladywood	47%
4.	Manchester Central	44%
5.	Birmingham, Hodge Hill	43%
6.	Edmonton	43%
7.	Westminster North	43%
8.	Tottenham	42%
9.	Hackney South and Shoreditch	42%
10.	Manchester, Gorton	42%
11.	East Ham	42%
12.	Birmingham, Hall Green	42%
13.	Glasgow Central	41%
14.	Hackney North and Stoke Newington	41%
15.	West Ham	41%
16.	Blackley and Broughton	40%

There is further evidence to highlight geographical inequalities in relation to health. The Office for National Statistics released data in 2014 that showed the extent of these health inequalities in relation to life expectancy. Some of the statistics from that report include the following:

The Office for National Statistics is the UK's largest independent producer of official statistics

- In 2010–12 male life expectancy at birth was highest in East Dorset (82.9 years) and lowest in Glasgow City (72.6 years).

- For females, life expectancy at birth was highest in Purbeck (86.6 years) and lowest in Glasgow City (78.5 years).

- Approximately 91% of baby boys in East Dorset and 94% of girls in Purbeck will reach their 65th birthday, if 2010–12 mortality rates persist throughout their lifetime.

- The comparable figures for Glasgow City are 75% for baby boys and 85% for baby girls.

- Life expectancy at age 65 was highest for men in Harrow, where they could expect to live for a further 20.9 years compared with only 14.9 years for men in Glasgow City.

- For women at age 65, life expectancy was highest in Camden (23.8 years) and lowest in Glasgow City (18.3 years).

> **TOP TIP**
>
> 'The Glasgow Effect': read the report published by the Glasgow Centre for Population Health that investigates why equally deprived UK cities experience different health outcomes: www.gcph.co.uk/assets/0000/0801/ GCPH_Briefing_Paper_25_for_web.pdf

Quick Test

1. What are the two key reasons given for working households to be in poverty?

2. What evidence is there to suggest that the gap between rich and poor continues to widen?

3. Give evidence to highlight the massive inequalities that exist in terms of wealth within London; you may want to refer to the information on socio-economic status.

4. Summarise the information on life expectancy; is there evidence to suggest that the health of people in Scotland is poorer than that of those living in England?

Theories of inequalities in the UK

Social explanations/theories

Social explanations of inequality are often related to the hierarchy of power in society and are linked to socio-economic status, gender and ethnicity. Such factors would suggest that those at the higher end of the scale are white, educated and male. Social explanations further highlight that inequality exists in two key areas – inequality of opportunity and inequality of conditions.

- Inequality of opportunity = life chances, that is health, education, crime.
- Inequality of conditions = income inequalities, that is wealth, housing, material goods.

There are two main social theories of inequality: functionalist theory and conflict theory.

Functionalist theory

Functionalists would suggest that it is necessary and desirable for inequalities to exist in order for society to survive. They would argue that inequalities exist as a direct result of certain occupations and positions in society requiring a higher level of training, education and expertise and should, as a result, gain greater rewards. According to this view therefore society operates as a meritocracy based on ability.

Conflict theory

Conflict theorists would argue however that inequality exists due to the dominance of one group in society over another. They would argue that opportunities for social mobility are often difficult due to the repressive nature of those operating at the higher end of society because of their significantly greater political and economic power.

Income inequalities

Low paid and part-time workers suffer high levels of poverty. The Joseph Rowntree Foundation found in 2013 that more than half of the 13 million people in the UK classed as living in poverty were actually employed. Although the National Minimum Wage rose to £6.50 per hour in 2014 for someone over the age of 21 it is still argued to be less than what is required to meet the cost of living in the UK. In these situations it is often harder to cope financially than being unemployed as some part-time workers may not be entitled to any benefits and find that they are worse off in work. The Living Wage Foundation further highlighted this when they calculated that £7.85 per hour (£9.15 per hour in London) is required to meet the basic cost of living, and they encourage employers to provide this.

This is further evidenced in the 'Health and Wellbeing Survey' carried out by NHS Greater Glasgow and Clyde in 2011. The survey found that those living in the poorest areas of Glasgow are still twice as likely to have no qualifications as those in other areas.

Homelessness

The majority of the UK public would acknowledge that employment is the key method to escaping poverty, however those that are homeless are disadvantaged because they have no corresponding address for employment applications and day-to-day survival is often more of a priority than finding a job.

A homeless man in Edinburgh

TOP TIP

The 'Longer Lives' website highlights premature death rates across England and compares areas with similar incomes and levels of health: http://healthierlives.phe.org.uk/topic/mortality

Individualistic explanations/theories

Individualist theories of inequality would suggest that it occurs as a direct result of the behaviour and lifestyle choices made by the individual. Individualists would argue that it is the responsibility of the individual to prevent themselves and their families from suffering inequality and they would discourage the government from providing too much support, arguing that when too much support is available individuals will relinquish responsibility and become reliant on welfare. They further argue that lifestyle choices of the individual are a direct cause of wealth and health inequalities, with the individuals who choose to smoke, consume excess alcohol, eat a poor diet and lead a sedentary lifestyle paying the price for those choices. Poor lifestyle choices in turn lead to poor health, which can have a long-term impact on the ability of people to be fit for work. As a result the gap between those at the higher end of society (rich/affluent) and those at the lower end continues to grow.

Again there is significant evidence to support this theory, however what we often see is that the two theories are interrelated, i.e. those making poor lifestyle choices that lead to health inequalities are often doing so as a result of their income inequalities.

Obesity

Official figures highlighted that primary school children from poorer areas were twice as likely as those from more affluent areas to be obese. In some of the poorest areas of the UK more than 25% of children were obese. Data gathered showed that 26.7% of year six pupils (final year of primary) living in the London borough of Southwark were found to be obese.

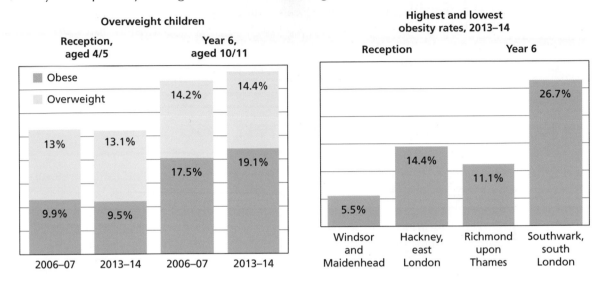

Overweight children

Reception, aged 4/5 — Year 6, aged 10/11

- Obese
- Overweight

	2006–07	2013–14	2006–07	2013–14
Overweight	13%	13.1%	14.2%	14.4%
Obese	9.9%	9.5%	17.5%	19.1%

Highest and lowest obesity rates, 2013–14

	Reception		Year 6
Windsor and Maidenhead	5.5%		
Hackney, east London	14.4%		
Richmond upon Thames		11.1%	
Southwark, south London			26.7%

In the poorest areas of Glasgow it was also noted that only a third of the population consume the recommended daily amount of five portions of fruit and veg and 30% of those living in the poorest areas have three 'unhealthy' habits such as smoking. It should be noted however that this is an improvement on the previous survey in 2008.

Smoking

Greater Glasgow and Clyde NHS report that although the numbers smoking in the poorest areas of Glasgow have dropped, it will take another 20 years before the figures are in line with the more affluent areas of the health board. This is concerning given that in Scotland, tobacco use is associated with over 13,000 deaths (around a quarter of all deaths) and around 56,000 hospital admissions every year.

Quick Test

1. What are the two main social explanations of inequality?
2. Outline the key points of the individualistic explanation of inequality.
3. 'Those living in the most deprived areas have poorer health as a result of their lifestyle choices'. Using the information on obesity and smoking, provide evidence to support the statement.

Impact of inequalities: gender inequalities

Inequality in society can have a devastating impact on a number of people, and these effects can range from a lower income to lower life expectancy. However there is clear evidence to suggest that some groups suffer greater effects with regard to their wealth and health than others. These groups may include children, the elderly, women and ethnic minorities. This section will focus on the impact of inequality on women and the next section will focus on ethnic minorities.

Gender inequalities: women and work

Official figures released by the UK government at the start of 2014 stated that the number of women in work was at its highest since 1971, making up 46% of the UK workforce. In Scotland, female employment was also at an all-time high with 71.4% of women in work, higher than the 68% of women in employment across the UK. It was reported in 2015 that Scotland's rate of female unemployment (4%) was the lowest in Europe, and also below the national rate of 5.3% However, even in work inequalities exist.

Gender pay gap

- The TUC published data in November 2013 that stated women working full time still earned, on average, £5000 per year less than men working full time and in some occupations the gap was as much as three times larger.

- The TUC have also found that 54% of women in part-time work are employed 'below their potential', that is they take jobs they are over-qualified for – this amounts to approximately 2.8 million women.

- The biggest gender pay gap was found to be amongst health professionals, with women earning £16,000 less than their male counterparts.

- The TUC also found that women earned less in 32 of the 35 major occupations outlined by the ONS.

- 70% of those working in minimum wage jobs are women.

Women further suffer inequality with regard to income in relation to childcare. Women are still the primary carers in society and by implication often have to take part-time work to balance having dependent children. Labour market statistics highlight that 82% of all men with dependent children work full time compared with only 30% of all women with dependent children, and only 6% of fathers with dependent children work part time compared to 37% of women with dependent children. This is a further issue in relation to the cost of childcare, with costs in the UK being the highest in the EU. Working families, on average, spend 26.6% of their income on childcare.

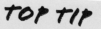

TOP TIP

Consider the management structure in your own school – is there a gender imbalance? Compare this to your primary school (most primary school head teachers in Scotland are women).

Discrimination

It is argued that sex discrimination, although outlawed by numerous pieces of legislation, continues to exist in the workplace, with women finding it difficult to achieve promotion or managerial/executive positions. For example:

- Women make up only 17% of board directors of FTSE 100 companies.
- The Fawcett Society estimated that each year 440,000 women fail to secure promotion due to pregnancy.

Women further find it difficult when trying to break into occupations that would give them a higher profile such as politics and the media.

- As of the 2015 general election, 191 of the 650 MPs in the House of Commons are women (29.4%).
- The Scottish Parliament (35%) and Welsh Assembly (40%) do better than Westminster, however the proportion of female representatives has fallen since those bodies were initially established.
- Under a quarter of reporters on daily national newspapers are female with only one female editor of a daily national: Dawn Neesom of the *Daily Star*.
- The Leveson Report criticised the way that women are portrayed in the media – some newspapers 'often failed to show consistent respect for the dignity and equality of women generally'.

Women make up only 17% of board directors of FTSE 100 companies

Female health

The ONS reports that females live longer than males but spend more time living with illness or disability, and further evidence highlighted a link between wealth and health in that teenage conception rates are highest in areas of deprivation. Alongside this NHS Health Scotland acknowledge that although men have a higher suicide rate than women, women are more likely to be admitted to hospital than men from self-harming, and 70% of patients given a diagnosis of 'anxiety or other related illness' by their GP were women. Deprivation is cited as the key factor in the existence of such inequalities.

Life expectancy figures suggest that health is improving with people living longer. However the life expectancy gap is an indicator of inequalities suffered by women due to geographical location: women, as well as men, can expect to live a significantly shorter life in certain locations.

Life expectancy

	Male	Female
Dorset	83 years	86.4 years
Glasgow City	72.6 years	78.4 years

Quick Test

1. How many women are estimated to be 'working below their potential'?
2. In which sector is the biggest gender pay gap found?
3. Do women suffer inequalities in relation to health? Give evidence to support your answer.

Impact of inequalities: ethnic inequalities

The 2011 census showed that the number of ethnic minorities living in the UK was an estimated 8 million, 14% of the population, with certain studies projecting numbers to double by 2050. However, when it comes to income, employment, education, housing and health, minorities suffer disproportionate inequality. This can be as a result of numerous factors ranging from prejudice and discrimination to lifestyle choices and deprivation.

Educational attainment

In June 2014 Manchester University published findings indicating that ethnic minorities have increased their overall educational attainment, with Chinese, Indian, Bangladeshi and black Africans performing better than whites when studying five or more GCSEs. The number of students gaining degrees by ethnic group highlights the improvement in educational attainment. However there is vast evidence to suggest that these improvements do not transfer to the workplace.

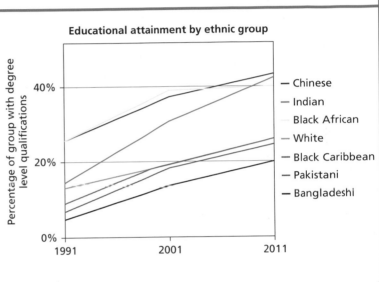

Educational attainment by ethnic group

- Chinese
- Indian
- Black African
- White
- Black Caribbean
- Pakistani
- Bangladeshi

Income inequalities

- Approximately 40% of all ethnic minorities live in low-income households, compared with 20% of the white population.
- There are inequalities within and between ethnic groups. The proportions who live in low-income households are:
  - 30% for Indians and black Caribbeans.
  - 50% for black Africans.
  - 60% for Pakistanis.
  - 70% for Bangladeshis.
- In all parts of the UK ethnic minorities, on average, are more likely to have lower incomes than whites. However there are greater differences in areas such as inner London, northern England and the Midlands, where high levels of ethnic minorities are concentrated. This is evident in unemployment rates as well as levels of ill health and inadequate housing.
- More than half of ethnic minorities living in London are on low incomes.

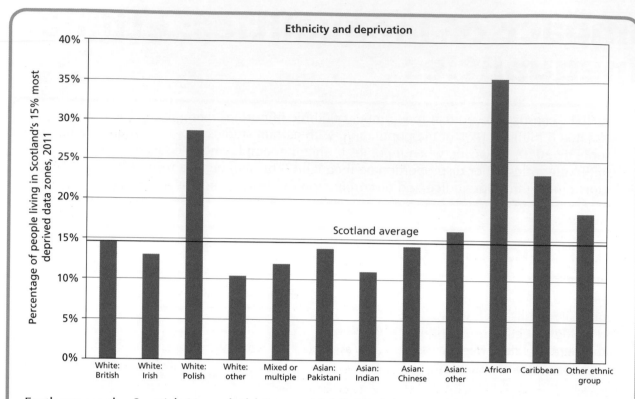

Furthermore the Scottish Household Survey highlighted that 'people from minority ethnic groups are less likely to be coping financially and more likely to have no savings'.

The graph provides further evidence of disproportionate inequalities among ethnic groups with over a third of people from an African background living in the most deprived areas of Scotland – highlighting the impact of low income on housing. In addition, it highlights that white Polish people, as well as those from Caribbean backgrounds and other ethnic groups, are suffering inequality.

Unemployment

Data released in February 2015 from the Annual Population Survey showed that the total rate of unemployment in the UK had decreased (standing at 6.2% overall), however it is evident from the table opposite that within and between ethnic groups there were significant inequalities in unemployment rates, with each non-white group having unemployment rates above the national average.

2013–14 unemployment rates

The table from the Annual Population Survey on the next page shows unemployment by ethnic background and age in the UK from October 2013 to September 2014.

	16—24		25—49		50+		Total (16+)	
	000s	Rate	000s	Rate	000s	Rate	000s	Rate
White	630	16%	740	5%	320	4%	1680	6%
Black	40	32%	70	13%	20	9%	130	15%
Asian	60	25%	100	8%	20	6%	180	10%
Other ethnic background	50	28%	50	8%	10	6%	110	11%
All ethnic backgrounds	770	17%	970	5%	360	4%	2090	6%

Source: Annual Population Survey data – http://www.parliament.uk

Notes: all numbers rounded to the nearest 10,000.

Asian includes Indian, Pakistani, Bangladeshi, and any other Asian ethnic background.

Other ethnic background includes Chinese, multiple ethnic and any other ethnic background.

Estimates based on survey responses so subject to sampling error.

Unemployment rate is the proportion of economically active people who are unemployed.

Health inequalities

Ethnic minority groups generally suffer poorer health than whites, however there are inequalities within and between ethnic groups. The UK government has published data suggesting that income and socio-economic position are the key factors relating to poor health. The Health Survey for England suggested that ethnic minorities report higher levels of poor health and also report poor health at a younger age than whites. These surveys also indicate that there are variations between ethnic groups with Pakistani, Bangladeshi and black Caribbean people reporting the poorest health, while Indians are on a par with white and Chinese people in reporting better health. When considering various illnesses and conditions, ethnic minorities report higher levels of cardio-vascular disease (CVD) but lower levels of cancer.

Case study: uptake of healthcare services
- Government data has shown that ethnic minorities are less likely to access hospital care, for example, South Asians have been found to have lower access to care for coronary heart disease.
- Fewer people in ethnic groups have stopped smoking than in white groups.
- The Healthcare Commission patient surveys have suggested that people from some ethnic groups are less satisfied with NHS services, for example South Asian patients report poorer experiences in hospitals.

Housing

Ethnic minorities tend to suffer inequalities in housing that subsequently lead to inequalities in health. The Race Equality Foundation found that around 15% of ethnic minorities in England lived in a house with at least one 'Category 1 hazard' (a severe threat to the health or safety of a resident), leading to subsequent health inequalities. A further study conducted by the University of Manchester has found that the UK's issues around securing housing have hit ethnic minorities the most, with minorities 'more likely to live in insecure, substandard and private rented accommodation'.

Securing housing is a concern for all, including ethnic minorities

Quick Test

1. What evidence is there to suggest that the educational attainment of ethnic minorities has improved?

2. Outline the key issues for ethnic minorities in relation to income and employment.

3. What do you think might constitute a Category 1 hazard with regard to housing?

Government response to inequalities

The UK has a long history of providing a comprehensive welfare state in order to protect the social and economic wellbeing of its citizens. This has involved the UK government's Department for Work and Pensions (DWP) and the devolved parliaments in Scotland, Wales and Northern Ireland introducing legislation, providing services in relation to health and education, as well as support given directly to individuals in the form of benefits.

Benefits

TOP TIP

Use the UK government website to research how the most recent budget will affect benefits allocated to different groups: www.gov.uk/browse/benefits

Unemployed: Job Seekers Allowance (JSA)

JSA is financial support given to those over the age of 18 who are actively seeking and are able for work. JSA also provides a work coach to help the claimant devise a work plan relating to how they are going to find a job. Claimants must attend a Jobcentre Plus office (usually every two weeks) to 'sign on' and inform the work coach of what they have been doing to seek employment, e.g. job applications and interviews. Failure to comply with the criteria may result in claimants having their JSA stopped.

Unemployed: Employment and Support Allowance (ESA)

Paid to those claimants who are ill or disabled and are unable to work. ESA is seen as personalised support so that there is help available to get the claimant back into work if possible. Claimants must attend 'Work Capability Assessments' while their claim is being assessed.

A Jobcentre Plus office where claimants attend a fortnightly meeting

The assessment establishes the extent to which claimants are unable to work and the amount awarded is dependent on their circumstances. Claimants must attend regular interviews with an advisor to set 'job goals' and look to improve their employability skills.

Low-income families

Working Tax Credit (WTC)

WTC is available to those who are:

- 16–24 and have a child or a qualifying disability.
- 25+ with or without children.

Claimants must work a certain number of hours per week but their income must fall below a certain level. It is all dependent on personal circumstances, but claimants could be eligible to claim up to £1940 a year.

Free school meals

Families in England and Wales claiming certain benefits (Income Support, Universal Credit, Child Tax Credit) may be eligible for free school meals for their children. In Scotland all primary 1–3 children, no matter the financial situation, are eligible for free school meals. This has affected around 165,000 children with parents saving up to £330 a year per child. This is regarded as more than a financial support and is viewed as an attempt by the Scottish Government to improve children's health by providing a nutritious, well-balanced meal each school day.

Child Benefit

Paid to parents as long as they don't have an income of over £50,000. The weekly payment is £20.70 for the eldest or only child, with £13.70 a week paid for each additional child.

Universal Credit

Universal Credit is part of the government's Welfare Reform strategy, replacing certain benefits (JSA, Housing Benefit, WTC, CTC, ESA, Income Support) with one single benefit in parts of the UK. Iain Duncan Smith (Secretary of State for Work and Pensions) has stated that it is an attempt to make welfare simpler, reduce fraud and get more people into work. Universal Credit is being phased in gradually, as of January 2015 it is being rolled out in Bath, Hammersmith, Harrogate, Inverness, Northwest England and Sutton. Claimants of Universal Credit are eligible to work and there is no limit to the number of hours worked – payment of Universal Credit will reduce the more they earn.

Iain Duncan Smith (Secretary of State for Work and Pensions)

In order to receive Universal Credit the claimant must accept a claimant commitment. This is an agreement that the claimant will do certain tasks, dependant on their health, responsibilities at home and how much help is needed to get to work.

Criticisms

Universal Credit has been heavily criticised by opposition political parties, anti-poverty campaigners and the media as a result of the change to a monthly payment, which claimants often find difficult to manage, and the many technical problems faced during the rollout period. The DWP originally promised to have one million people on Universal Credit by April 2014, however the rollout was delayed a number of times. A DWP report published in October 2014 showed that only 14,170 were claiming. By May 2015 over 100,000 people had made a claim, and this is expected to rise to 500,000 by May 2016.

Chris Bryant, shadow Welfare Reform Minister in 2014, noted that 100,000 was only 1% of the expected number of claimants and an estimated £130 million had already been spent on Universal Credit, and that further delays would be costly.

The National Audit Office further criticised the introduction of Universal Credit given that it is estimated that it will cost £2.8 billion in staffing due to the reliance on existing IT systems to roll it out nationwide, rather than switching to a digital service.

Disability Living Allowance (DLA)

DLA is the benefit given to people aged between 16 and 64 who are disabled. It is gradually being replaced by the Personal Independence Payment (PIP). PIP aims to help with the extra costs caused by long-term ill health or a disability. It may also be paid to claimants who need help looking after themselves, have daily living difficulties or have walking difficulties. Daily living difficulties might include:

- Preparing or eating food
- Washing and bathing
- Dressing/undressing
- Reading and communicating
- Managing medicines
- Making decisions about money

The rate paid depends on how their condition affects an individual not the condition itself. Claimants undergo an assessment to work out the level of support to be given. The rate is regularly reassessed to ensure accurate support is being given and to attempt to avoid benefit fraud.

Elderly

State Pension

This is a regular financial payment once people reach state pension age (currently 65, or 60 for some women). Pensioners can receive up to £113.10 per week, depending on previous income and National Insurance contributions made. However the government guarantees households a minimum income of £148.35 for a single person or £226.50 for a couple. To make up the difference between the State Pension and the minimum income guarantee pensioners can apply for other benefits to top up their state pension, including Pension Credit.

Elderly benefit payments include the State Pension

Winter Fuel Payment

An annual payment of between £100 and £300 tax-free to help pay for heating bills. Most payments are made automatically between November and December and if the claimant receives the State Pension they should automatically be sent a Winter Fuel Payment.

Other benefits

The following benefits may be available to different groups:

- Income Support
- Housing Benefit
- Council Tax Benefit
- Free bus travel
- Free TV licence
- Child Tax Credit
- Sure Start Maternity Grant
- Cold Weather Payment
- Education Maintenance Allowance

Benefit cap

As part of the UK government's 'austerity measures', they introduced a 'benefits cap' in 2013. This placed a limit on the total amount of benefits that most people aged 16–64 can claim:

- £500 a week for couples (with or without children living with them).
- £500 a week for a single parent (children living with them).
- £350 a week for a single adult (no children or children don't live with them).

Benefit claimants often find this confusing as there are a number of exceptions, e.g. you would not be affected by this cap if anyone in your home qualifies for Working Tax Credit or other benefits including DLA, ESA or PIP.

The Smith Commission and welfare proposals

The Commission proposed that a range of disability benefits, including Disability Living Allowance/Personal Independent Payments should be devolved to the Scottish Parliament. Around 343,000 people receive Disability Living Allowance in Scotland alone, so a relatively substantial number of people may be affected by any future changes to this benefit.

The Smith Commission also proposes that Scotland should have:

- Powers to vary the housing element of Universal Credit.
- Administrative power to change the frequency of Universal Credit payments, vary the existing plans for single household payments and pay landlords direct for housing costs.
- Powers to create new benefits in devolved areas and to 'top-up' reserved benefits.

Reaction to the Smith Commission proposals on welfare has been mixed. For example, while some have welcomed the proposals others have suggested they are a piecemeal approach to the devolution of further powers on welfare.

Means testing

Certain benefits are classed as **universal** – this means everyone is entitled to them no matter their financial situation. Until 2013 every family received child benefit, however since then families where one parent earns more than £50,000 a year are unable to claim. This is what is referred to as means testing – claimants must declare the amount of income and capital they have, which then affects eligibility to claim. Means testing is regularly criticised on the basis that it is often complicated and costly to assess whether someone is entitled to benefits. Furthermore it is argued that due to means testing a number of often needy recipients do not claim what they are entitled to, due to the complex nature of the application form or simply because they are unaware that they are entitled to further support. As a result billions go unclaimed. In 2012 it was estimated that up to £2.8 billion in Pension Credit alone was not taken up. As a result, Age UK has called for the government to make people more aware of what they are entitled to. The DWP stated further that up to 620,000 people failed to claim up to £2 billion in Income Support or Employment Support Allowance, as well up to 1.1 million people failing to claim £3.1 billion in Housing Benefit.

TOP TIP

Use the UK government website to review further benefits available to UK citizens: www.gov.uk/browse/benefits

Quick Test

1. Outline the support offered to those claiming JSA.
2. Explain why ESA is often referred to as 'personalised support'.
3. What should be the benefits of Universal Credit? List three criticisms of Universal Credit.
4. What did the introduction of the benefits cap mean for those claiming financial support?
5. Explain what you understand by the term 'means tested'.

Attempts to reduce health inequalities

Smoking ban

The ban on smoking in public places had a key aim: to reduce passive smoking. Scotland introduced the ban first, in March 2006, followed by Wales and Northern Ireland in April 2007, with England introducing the ban in July 2007. Researchers from Action on Smoking and Health stated that it was an important move in improving public health and was popular amongst the British public. A recent poll on support for the smoking ban demonstrated that almost 80% of people in the UK support it.

Since March 2006, smoking has been banned in all enclosed public places in Scotland

Health promotion campaigns

This web page lists a range of policies and strategies implemented by both the UK and Scottish governments to promote an individual approach to a healthy lifestyle: www.patient.co.uk/directory/health-promotion-lifestyle

Eat Better Feel Better

This is a Scottish Government health promotion website that encourages healthy eating and a healthy lifestyle: www.eatbetterfeelbetter.co.uk

Change 4 Life

A UK government strategy to provide families with ideas, recipes and advice on how to live and eat well: www.nhs.uk/Change4Life/Pages/why-change-for-life.aspx

The UK and Scottish governments have campaigns to encourage people to eat healthily

Screening programmes/HPV vaccine

Screening programmes and vaccinations are seen as a method of preventing future illness or identifying a killer disease early. Breast cancer is the most common cancer in Scottish women, accounting for 28.9% of female cancer cases. There were 4457 new cases diagnosed in women in Scotland in 2010 and 1022 deaths from the disease in 2010. The Scottish Breast Screening Programme invites women aged between 50 and 70 for screening every three years. For women diagnosed with breast cancer, finding the disease early gives the best chance of successful treatment.

The human papillomavirus (HPV) vaccine for girls aged 11 to 13 years helps protect against cervical cancer. The HPV vaccine is offered to girls at secondary schools across Scotland.

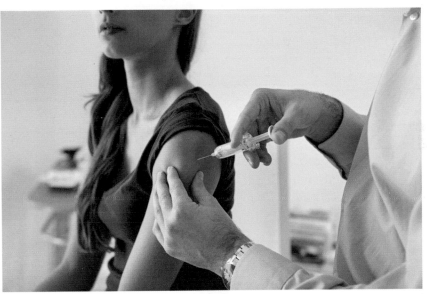

The human papillomavirus (HPV) vaccine helps protect against cervical cancer.

TOP TIP

Watch some of the short films on NHS Scotland's YouTube channel to identify other strategies to reduce health inequalities: www.youtube.com/user/NHSHealthScotland

Quick Test

1. What are two key benefits of screening programmes and vaccinations?
2. Watch some videos on NHS Scotland's YouTube channel and identify three other strategies to reduce health inequalities in Scotland.

Government legislation to reduce inequalities

National Minimum Wage (NMW)

This is a legally-binding minimum rate of pay, introduced in the UK in 1999. The Labour government introduced it in a bid to combat poverty. However, the Living Wage Foundation argue that it is not sufficient and should be increased. Evidence provided earlier in the book suggests that even those earning the minimum wage are still living below the poverty line. The rates as of October 2015 are:

21+	£6.70
18–20	£5.30
Under 18	£3.87
Apprentice*	£3.30

*This rate is for apprentices aged 16 to 18 and those aged 19 or over who are in their first year. All other apprentices are entitled to the National Minimum Wage for their age.

In 2015, Chancellor George Osborne announced that the government would be introducing a new 'National Living Wage' from April 2016 of £7.20 an hour for those aged over 25. This will rise to over £9 an hour by 2020.

Equality Act (2010)

The Act legally protects people from discrimination in the workplace and wider society in an attempt to reduce inequalities. The Act replaced previous anti-discrimination laws with a single Act, making the law easier to understand and strengthening protection in some situations.

The Act states that it is unlawful to discriminate against anyone because of:

- Age
- Transgender
- Marriage/civil partnership
- Pregnancy
- Gender
- Ethnicity
- Sexual orientation
- Disability

It protects citizens in a number of situations including the workplace, education, using public services and buying or renting property.

Laws replaced by the Act include:

- Sex Discrimination Act (1975)
- Race Relations Act (1976)
- Disability Discrimination Act (1995)

Maternity and paternity leave/pay

This ensures that employment rights are granted when on maternity leave, such as the right to pay rises, accruing holiday entitlement and the right to return to work. Legislation ensures that women are entitled to 52 weeks statutory maternity leave with statutory maternity pay being paid for 39 weeks.

Fathers are also guaranteed the opportunity to take paid leave on the birth of their children. Fathers are entitled to one or two weeks ordinary leave and up to 26 weeks paid additional paternity leave but only if the mother or co-adopter returns to work.

Fathers can also take paid leave when they have a baby

Quick Test

1. When was the NMW introduced, and what was its key aim?
2. What evidence is there to suggest that the NMW has not met its key aim?
3. Outline the key aims of the Equality Act (2010).
4. Explain how this Act has impacted on paternity leave/pay.

The role of the law in society

Rights and responsibilities

In the UK it is accepted that everyone is given legal rights, by law, and alongside these exist responsibilities; for example we have the right to free speech when supporting a particular cause, however it is our responsibility not to make false or damaging statements against someone or an organisation. This would be regarded as slander, which is a criminal offence.

The law is therefore important in society in that it offers guidance and a set of norms with regard to behaviour. People will abide by the law as they are aware of the consequences of breaking the law. Without law, conflicts between individuals and groups would arise and it is argued society would be chaotic and anarchy would ensue. However, even with a robust system of law in place there is a constant need for the law to act, with the court system ruling on many different areas of criminal activity.

The role of the police

Police forces in the UK have a number of key functions:

- To maintain law and order.
- To protect members of the public and their property.
- To prevent crime.
- To reduce the fear of crime.
- To improve the quality of life of all citizens.

Police officers are also required to carry out certain tasks in relation to their work, such as attending community council meetings, submitting reports to the Procurator Fiscal's office in relation to criminal activity (Scotland), and they often have to attend court to give evidence.

Police officers carry out a variety of tasks

In 2012 the Scottish Government approved legislation to establish the Scottish Police Authority and Police Service of Scotland, known as 'Police Scotland', replacing the eight police forces that had existed formerly. The 17,000 strong force became the second largest force in the UK, after the Metropolitan Police in London. Stephen House, formerly of Strathclyde Police, was appointed as Chief Constable of the new unified force.

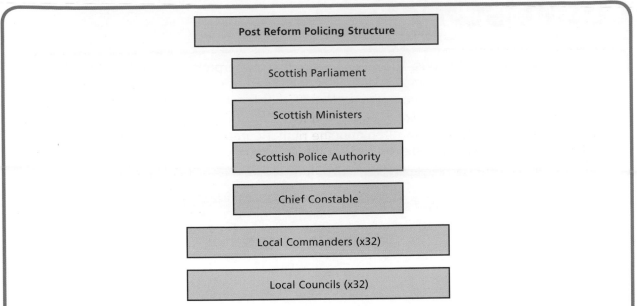

The new policing structure

There were a number of reasons given for this reform including cost effectiveness, with a reported estimate of £47 million savings on officer costs within five years. However critics saw the radical move as being driven purely by savings rather than by a desire to streamline the police force. Furthermore critics viewed having only one Chief Constable as being susceptible to interference from the government, possibly leading to their having limited autonomy in decision making.

The Scottish Police Authority was set up to hold the Chief Constable to account for the policing of Scotland. Chairman of the board, businessman Vic Emery, said that the SPA would be a mechanism to 'scrutinise, test and approve' police decisions.

Although there is only one single force it can be divided into three separate branches – uniform, criminal investigation (CID) and traffic. Specialised branches are also deployed at certain times, for example dog, mounted, underwater and community.

TOP TIP

Read this article in the *Herald* to gain a broader understanding of the pros and cons of a single police force: www.heraldscotland.com/comment/herald-view/pros-and-cons-of-a-single-police-force.14716825

Quick Test

1. Outline the main roles of the police.
2. Explain, in detail, why the police force in Scotland was reformed to establish one force.
3. Why was the Scottish Police Authority set up?

Court structure

In the UK the system of courts, known as the judiciary, interprets and applies the law in the name of the state. It is complicated in that the UK does not exist as a single body – Scotland and Northern Ireland operate under different legal arrangements than those in place in England and Wales. One feature that is common to all is the Supreme Court – the highest court of appeal. The law often appears further complicated as there are different legal pathways for different types of dispute.

The Supreme Court building entrance in London

Civil law

Civil law is concerned with the interrelationships and conflicts between different individuals and groups. Civil cases may involve matters such as disputes over wills or contracts. Cases brought to court under civil law are usually done so by individuals rather than the state and might often result in compensation being paid to the victim rather than a prison sentence.

Criminal law

Criminal law deals with crimes committed by an individual or group – violent behaviour, serious fraud, burglary, etc. Such cases are normally brought to court by the state and could lead to large fines or imprisonment.

TOP TIP

Research recent cases where the Supreme Court has heard appeals on behalf of Scottish prisoners. Can you think why the Scottish Government would be unhappy about this?

Court structure

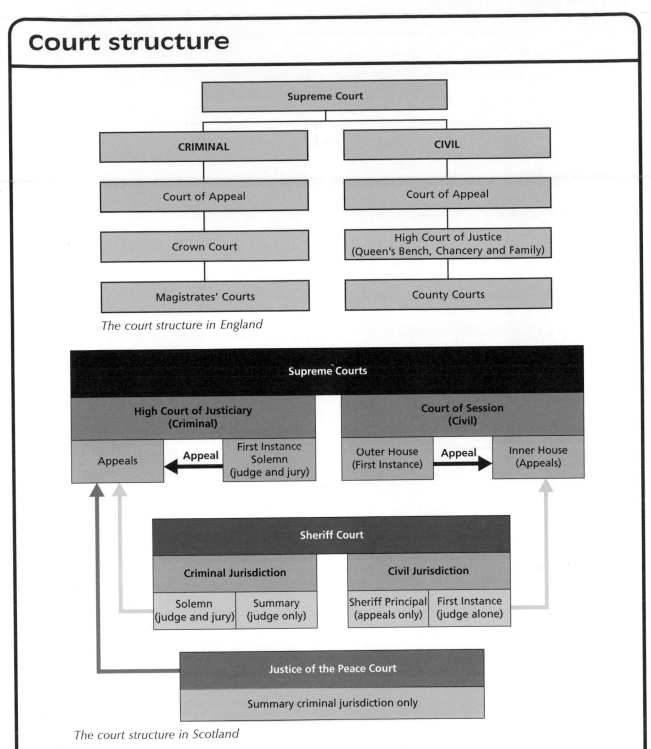

The court structure in England

The court structure in Scotland

Courts in Scotland have two different legal procedures: solemn and summary (see figure above). Solemn procedures involve the most serious criminal cases. These cases may lead to a trial, with a jury, in either the High Court or Sheriff Court. Summary cases on the other hand are less serious offences. Trials are conducted without a jury and may be heard in either the Sheriff Court or in a Justice of the Peace Court. One further difference that sets Scottish criminal courts apart is that they have three possible verdicts as opposed to two: guilty, not guilty and not proven.

The Scottish courts system

This table shows what each court can do in Scotland:

High Court of Justiciary	Highest criminal court in Scotland, dealing with the most serious of crimes: treason, murder and rape, armed robbery, drug trafficking and sexual offences involving children.	• Unlimited maximum fine • Unlimited maximum prison sentence
Sheriff Court	Deals with cases too serious for the Justice of the Peace courts but not serious enough for the High Court. Depending on evidence given in relation to a case the Sheriff can refer a case to the High Court.	Summary • Maximum fine £5000 • Maximum prison sentence 12 months Solemn • Unlimited maximum fine • Maximum prison sentence five years (or pass to High Court) • Sheriffs can also issue alternatives to prison as well as more specific punishments, such as bans from social media such as Facebook and Twitter
Justice of the Peace Court	Lowest level of criminal court. Hears cases of breach of the peace, minor assaults, minor road traffic offences and petty theft.	• Maximum fine £2500 • Maximum prison sentence 60 days

Quick Test

1. Why do we regard the law as an important function of our society?
2. Explain why the UK court system is often referred to as 'complicated'.
3. Outline the difference between solemn and summary cases.

The penal system in Scotland

The Scottish Prison Service (SPS) is a Scottish government agency and was established in 1993.

The Scottish Prison Service

The purpose of the service is to maintain secure custody and good order within prisons, whilst caring for prisoners with humanity and delivering opportunities that give the best chance to reduce reoffending once a prisoner returns to the community. The SPS has 13 publicly managed prisons and two privately managed prisons.

It is widely acknowledged and accepted that certain individuals require a custodial sentence for a variable period of time, dependent on the crime for which they have been convicted. Supporters of prison would argue that it acts as a deterrent from committing crime or further crimes on release as well as a measure of ensuring public safety. Critics of prison however refer to the increasing cost of holding a prisoner for any length of time and the overcrowding within prisons. Furthermore the high levels of reoffending suggest that prison does not always achieve its aims. Calls for alternatives to custodial sentences are often sought.

Alternatives to prison

Alternatives to custody are often referred to as **community sentencing**. Scotland is regarded as having one of the most extensive ranges of alternatives to custody in Europe. The most commonly used alternatives to custody are listed below.

Probation
Probation is the most frequently used community sentence. The main purpose of probation is to work with offenders to prevent or reduce their reoffending by providing opportunities for rehabilitation. Probation Orders can be used very flexibly by the courts and additional conditions can be attached to them, for example requiring the offender to undertake unpaid work, or imposing an electronic tag.

Community Payback Orders
An offender given a community payback order is required to carry out unpaid work of benefit to the community for between 20 and 300 hours.

Restriction of Liberty Orders (tagging)

RLOs restrict offenders, who must be 16 or over, to a particular place or places for up to 12 hours per day for up to 12 months.

Drug Treatment and Testing Orders

DTTOs offer drug treatment and testing with regular reviews by the courts. These target people whose offending is linked to their drug problem, for example those who steal to fund their drug habit. The intention of a DTTO is to help offenders overcome a drug addiction, thereby reducing or eliminating the need to reoffend.

Quick Test

1. List the key arguments for and against custodial sentences.
2. Outline the main alternatives to prison issued by Scottish courts.

Theories of crime

Individualist theories of crime

Individualist theories of crime relate generally to three key areas:

- Genetic theories
- Biological theories
- Psychological theories

Genetic theories

Cesare Lombroso (1876) identified that criminals had a number of similar characteristics:

- Large jaw
- High cheekbones
- Large ears
- Insensitivity to pain

However, Lombroso was heavily criticised because his research was taking place only in Italian prisons at a time when inmates were mainly poor and their physical appearance had been affected by the levels of deprivation from which they had suffered, alongside a poor diet. He was further criticised as not everyone who commits a crime ends up in prison.

Sheldon & Eleanor Glueck, researchers working in the early to mid-1900s, identified relationships between physical build and 'delinquent' behaviour in males; delinquent referring here to deviant or criminal behaviour. Features of such 'delinquents' included a stocky, rounded build and being more active and aggressive. These researchers were criticised because what some people might see as 'active, aggressive delinquent' behaviour, others may not.

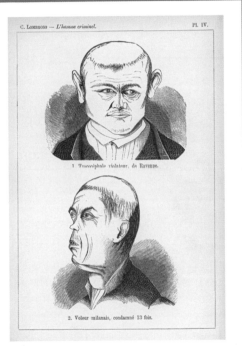

Illustrations from Lombroso's work

Y chromosome theory

Key features of this theory are:

- Extra Y chromosome.
- XYY chromosome makeup rather than XY.
- Studies in Denmark have indicated that men found with the extra Y chromosome were more frequently convicted of sexual abuse, arson and burglary.

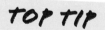

TOP TIP

Use www.sociology.org.uk to support your understanding of theories of crime.

The study acknowledged that the increase in crime rate may also have been related to deprivation and poor socio-economic conditions.

Biological/psychological theories

Key features of these theories are:

- Crime is a form of illness.
- The criminal cannot help but commit crime.
- Result of a chemical imbalance in the brain.
- Born criminal.

Such theories are often based on the idea of **nature versus nurture**. Many murderers throughout history have had no real explanation for their criminal behaviour and theorists would argue they have an inherent impulse to kill. However those who would support the **nurture** theory argue that criminals are not born this way; they are conditioned by society and environmental factors. There have been a number of studies carried out in an attempt to support such biological/psychological theories.

Adoption studies

Sarnoff A. Mednick analysed court convictions with 14,000 adoptees among them. Of these, he analysed the criminal records of both their adoptive parents and biological parents and found evidence to support the fact that those with biological parents who had criminal records were more likely to commit crime even when their adoptive parents had no criminal records. Further studies conducted in the US found that children born to incarcerated women, who were later adopted, were more likely to offend in later life. In Denmark research highlighted a biological component for criminal acts against property – those whose biological fathers had been convicted of property crimes were more likely to engage in similar behaviour.

Further research would suggest that criminals often have specific personality traits or disorders. Eysenck highlighted that criminals often displayed 'extrovert' behaviour, that is, they acted impulsively, craved excitement and took risks. However such theories have been criticised because people do not tend to behave in **one** particular way at all times. Some personality disorders originate in childhood. Attention deficit hyperactivity disorder (ADHD) and oppositional defiance disorder (ODD) are two common disorders that prisoners report having in their childhood, which have followed them into adulthood. Psychologists often argue that childhood experiences have a direct impact on criminal activity in later life.

Some research has found that children whose parents have criminal records are more likely to commit crime

Case study: Joanna Dennehy

Joanna Dennehy became the first woman in the UK to be sentenced to a full life term by a judge due to the nature of her crimes. One year prior to her committing these crimes she had been diagnosed with a personality disorder and was accused of lacking the normal range of human emotions.

Joanna Dennehy

Quick Test

1. What are the key features of a criminal as identified by Lombroso?
2. Outline the key features of the nature versus nurture debate?
3. Summarise the key arguments and criticisms of individualist theories of crime.

Social explanations of crime

Three key explanations of crime will be discussed here, however you may have covered other theories in class.

Functionalist theory

Two key theories will be outlined under this heading – **strain theory** and **social control theory**.

Strain theory

According to strain theory, people become stressed or strained over a particular situation and as a result commit crime. It is argued that they engage in crime as a means to escape the particular stress or strain they are experiencing. A person may be stressed as a result of losing their job and being reliant on benefits and as a result steal to maintain the lifestyle to which they have become accustomed. On the other hand it may be that the crime is in revenge for a previous crime that has caused stress or strain to that person or a family member. Agnew identifies two key types of strain:

Father kills thief who took son's phone

Derek Grant used an iPhone app to trace his son's mugger then stabbed him to death in a knife fight, court hears.

In August 2014 Derek Grant admitted killing Patrick Bradley, who had stolen his son's iPhone

- Others preventing you from achieving your goals.
- Others taking things you value, which creates negative stimuli.

Strain theory can be related to the failure to achieve desired goals. Agnew links crime with failing to achieve desired goals: money and status for adults, and autonomy from adults for young people. The theory suggests that the further away you are from achieving the goal, the more likely that under strain you will commit a crime in order to move closer to the goal or desire.

Social control theory

Unlike strain theorists, who consider what pushes people into crime, control theorists look for reasons why most people conform in society. Control theorists such as Hirschi argue that there are three major types of social control that prevent people from committing crime:

- **Direct control** – family members, school teachers, work colleagues, the police.
- **Stake in conformity** – those with a lot to lose will fear being caught; this may be due to the emotional attachment to family or perhaps the attachment they have to society; people who have invested their time and effort in growing a business and developing a positive reputation are less likely to risk losing this through crime.
- **Internal control** – relates to the beliefs/values and self-control a person has; the more self-control an individual has, the less likely they are to engage in crime.

Social learning theory

Key features of this theory are:

- Crime occurs as a result of association with others – family/peer group.
- Learned behaviour – negative role models.
- Crime is viewed as desirable or justifiable in certain situations.
- The most obvious reason would be peer relations – a theory supported by the ever-growing number of gangs in the UK. However crime can occur without any direct contact with others – evidence of growth in individual criminal activity is linked to engagement with particular films, mass media, computer games.

Rioting in London in 2011

The London riots of August 2011 are a key example of when crime was viewed by many as justifiable. Others simply joined in along with their peers.

Interactionist theory – labelling theory

Theorists would argue that continued crime can be a consequence of official efforts to control crime. Once a criminal has been arrested, prosecuted and punished they have been labelled a criminal. This then reinforces the fact that they have a different position in society to others and often prevents them from moving away from criminal activity. A criminal record may prevent someone from getting a particular job and in order to survive that person may continue to engage in crime, as they perceive themselves to be worth nothing better. John Braithwaite argued that although this could be true for some, it might not be the case for all. He argued that in some situations crime would decrease as a result of reintegration into society – the criminal who feels ashamed or guilty for their actions, or the criminal who has been forgiven by his family or peer group may not feel the need or urge to engage in further criminal activity.

> **TOP TIP**
>
> Do some research: use online newspapers to find criminal activity that could be argued to have occurred as a result of **labelling**.

Quick Test

1. What are the two key theories that come under the heading of functionalist theory?
2. Outline the three measures of social control offered by Hirschi.
3. Summarise the key features of social learning theory.

The impact of crime on society: economic

Crime not only leads to numerous financial and emotional costs for those who have been victims, but crime also forces local and national governments to spend billions on the prevention of crime and the detection, prosecution and punishment of criminals. We can therefore argue that there are economic consequences of crime for the individual, the taxpayer and the government.

The rising costs of crime

Violent crime costs the UK economy £124 billion, report suggests

Violent crime costs the UK economy more than £124 billion a year, equivalent to £4700 for every household, a study out today has revealed.

The rising costs of crime

Reports in the *Telegraph* and the *Guardian* in 2013 highlighted the rising cost of crime in the UK. The actual financial cost of violent crime equalled 7.7% of UK GDP, which included the cost of police investigations, courts and prison expenditure. In 2012 murder alone was estimated to have cost the country £1.3 billion, with retail crime costing the UK economy £1.6 billion, an increase of 15.6% since 2011. This was attributed to the sector being targeted by serious, organised criminals. A report by the British Retail Consortium indicated that one in 20 shops in the UK suffered a robbery in 2012, with the average cost to the retailer tripling from £989 to £3005.

TOP TIP

For further information on the economic impact of crime read the following articles: www.telegraph.co.uk/news/10013830/Violent-crime-costs-the-UK-economy-124-billion-report-suggests.html and www.theguardian.com/business/2013/jan/21/cost-retail-crime-rises

The economic impact of the London riots

- David Cameron announced a £10 million recovery fund and a £20 million pledge from the government for high street recovery. The estimated cost of the clean-up was £43.5 million.
- Forty-five homes in Tottenham alone were lost to fire. The estimated damage to property was £300 million.
- Government support was given to insurers to cover the cost of claims.
- The Sony warehouse was destroyed and thousands of DVDs, CDs and computer games ruined. As a result the Arctic Monkeys could only release their new album online as no physical copies survived.
- Local convenience stores were looted for alcohol and cigarettes, whilst sports chains were robbed of clothing and footwear and £80 million was lost in sales.
- Police from Wales and Scotland were called in to help out the forces in London. Police numbers in the capital were nearly tripled from 6000 to 16,000.

As a consequence of the above, some businesses closed altogether, leading to unemployment. Insurers, in a bid to regain the cost of claims, increased their premiums for the following year.

After the London riots, some businesses closed altogether

Quick Test

1. What does crime force local and national governments to do that leads to growing financial burden?
2. Why was there such a rise in the cost of crime for the retail sector?

The impact of crime on society: social

Crime not only has economic consequences but communities are often labelled as dangerous and recognised for their high crime rate as opposed to positive factors. As a result, crime in these communities often becomes commonplace and so they continue to suffer the consequences of crime. The negative impact continues further as fear in these communities gradually rises, with residents becoming 'withdrawn, defenseless and less committed to their communities' (source: http://law.jrank.org/pages/12125/Economic-Social-Effects-Crime.html). The value of housing decreases, with fewer businesses willing to invest in the area. Public opinion would often suggest that these types of communities are areas with high levels of deprivation, however there are a number of more affluent areas where crime rates are significant.

Case Study 1: Glasgow – 'the UK's most violent area'

In 2012, there were 2.7 homicides per 100,000 people in Glasgow

In 2013 Glasgow was given the title of the UK's most violent area based on a study conducted by the UK Peace Index (Institute for Economics and Peace). The study looked at 10 areas and highlighted Glasgow as being 'the least peaceful major urban centre', with the highest rates of homicide and violent crime. In 2012, there were 2.7 homicides per 100,000 people in Glasgow. This compares to 1.67 per 100,000 in London and a rate of 1.0 per 100,000 across the UK as a whole. The study attributed Glasgow's rating to the continued problem with alcohol abuse, knife crime and gangs. It further highlighted the fact that Glasgow has high levels of poverty and deprivation and concluded that there was a direct relationship between the two. However the study did acknowledge that over the last 10 years crime has decreased in Glasgow, with homicides down by 40% and violent crime down by 30%. London and Belfast came second and third in the study.

Further impact
- Lack of facilities in the area.
- A reduction in potential job opportunities.
- Social exclusion – crime culture accepted.
- Poor reputation.

Case Study 2: Manchester – an area of affluence

A survey of home insurance claims in Britain found that a suburb of Manchester known for its bohemian reputation was named the theft capital of the UK. One in 11 households in the M21 postcode area around Chorlton-cum-Hardy had made a claim for theft. The report further highlighted that highly affluent areas such as Roundhay in Leeds, and Gerrards Cross, Buckinghamshire, were susceptible to crime. These areas were named alongside more deprived areas that are often linked with crime such as Brixton, south London.

TOP TIP

Create a mind map to help you analyse the social impact of crime.

Impact of crime on the victim

Crime affects people in many different ways, whether it be in the short- or long-term. Victim Support reports that how people react to crimes will depend on each individual and on the following factors:

- The type of crime.
- Whether the victim knows the person who committed the crime.
- The support that the victim gets (or doesn't get) from family, friends, the police and others.
- Things that have happened in the past (because if the victim has had to deal with difficult events before, they may have found ways of coping).

Victim Support state that certain emotions such as anger or fear are common after being the victim of a crime, however some victims appear to suffer no immediate impact, feeling 'normal' for a while and then experiencing some form of anxiety at a later date. As a result of the anxiety or fear, perhaps having been the victim of an unprovoked attack or more seriously a sexual assault, victims can sometimes suffer physical symptoms such as lack of sleep, depression or, at the most extreme, feeling compelled to take their own lives because they are unable to cope with the pressures and mental strain of what has happened to them. This may be true of victims who feel vulnerable or powerless, especially where the crime is on-going, for example in cases of domestic abuse or racial violence. In 2009 Fiona Pilkington took her own life as well as her disabled daughter's life after contacting police more than 30 times about claims of abuse from members of a gang in the community where she lived. She had claimed that the group continually verbally abused her family as well as vandalising her home. Police were accused of failing to act on these reports and considered them as merely anti-social behaviour.

PC David Rathband

Victims of crime may also suffer varying levels of economic impact. Should the victim have suffered extreme physical injury they may not be able to return to their previous occupation. In the case of PC David Rathband (above), being shot and blinded by Raoul Moat in 2010 had the most serious impact possible. PC Rathband was unable to return to his traffic police job as a result of his injuries and struggled to cope with his immediate and irreparable disabilities – 20 months after the attack he killed himself.

Quick Test

1. What factors affect how individuals react to being victims of crime?
2. In the case of Fiona Pilkington, could it be argued that the police were partly to blame? Explain your answer.
3. In what circumstances would victims perhaps suffer an economic consequence of crime?

The impact of crime on the offender

Crime and the offender

The impact of crime on the offender varies, again generally depending on the crime committed. For instance the impact of using illegal drugs on a recreational basis could lead to a criminal record as well as the potential development of a drug habit, with many drug addicts resorting to further crimes, such as shoplifting, to fund their addiction. Criminals in these situations will often find it hard, if not impossible, to hold down a job; the further consequence of a criminal record being the impact it has on future employment. Furthermore, whilst taking drugs many addicts find a major deterioration in their physical and mental health, with some facing the most extreme situations, for example contracting HIV through the sharing of needles or death as a result of an overdose.

The CRB holds records of criminal activity

Alongside this the majority of employers will ask about previous convictions and 4 million Criminal Records Bureau (CRB) checks are carried out every year in England and Wales. There are a growing number of professions where criminal records are never lifted, such as doctors, nurses, teachers, police officers and lawyers. Anyone applying to study specific courses in the health, social care and education fields will be subject to scrutiny. If found to have a criminal conviction it is likely that their application will be refused, leading to limited opportunities for educational progression.

Criminal convictions may also impact on the ability to travel – difficulties will be encountered when applying for visas to enter certain countries. In order to gain entry into the USA for instance the visitor must declare all convictions and each case is dealt with on an individual basis.

Convicted criminals may also suffer in relation to housing. Criminals who are given a prison sentence may ultimately have to give up their property and may end up homeless on release due to some prisoners finding that family relationships break down as a result of a prison sentence. Furthermore, when applying for a mortgage, convictions must be declared – this may have an impact on your suitability for a loan.

Finally it is evident that there can be psychological implications to having a criminal record – notably shame and embarrassment.

Quick Test

1. Describe how the taking of drugs recreationally can lead to a far greater negative impact on the offender than crime alone.
2. Which professions are you prevented from working in if you have a criminal conviction?
3. List three ways that life may be affected as a result of having a criminal record.

Measures to tackle crime and their effectiveness

> *'Crime must be reduced and prevented to ensure people feel safe in their homes and communities. The government supports visible, responsive and accountable policing by empowering the public and freeing up the police to fight crime.'*
>
> *gov.uk/government/topics/crime-and-policing*

Tackling crime in England and Wales

The Crime Survey for England and Wales (CSEW) found that between September 2013 and September 2014 there were 7 million 'incidents' (anything reported to the police, including road traffic offences, disorderly behaviour – some not regarded as severe enough to be formally recorded), a decrease of 11% on the previous year. There were 3.7 million 'police recorded incidents' (crimes that would warrant a trial by jury and are listed on the 'notable offence' list – murder, kidnapping, racially aggravated assault, etc.), which was similar to the previous year. However the number of violent

Crime prevention measures reduce crime rates across local communities

crimes and sexual offences recorded increased. The Office for National Statistics argue that this is due to better recording of offences.

In the UK it is the responsibility of the Home Office to prevent crime in England and Wales and to ensure that measures are effectively taken to reduce crime rates across local communities. The UK government has adopted a new approach to tackling crime that shifts the power from Whitehall to local communities.

In March 2013 the UK government introduced a 'Reducing and Preventing Crime' strategy for England and Wales.

Measures to reduce crime include those listed below:

- Creating community triggers which will give victims and communities the right to demand that persistent antisocial behaviour is dealt with. Victims will be able to demand a review of their case and be assured that agencies such as the police and local authorities are working together to tackle the problem.
- Community safety partnerships (CSPs) are made up of representatives from the 'responsible authorities', which are:
  - police
  - local authorities
  - fire and rescue authorities

- ◦ probation service
- ◦ health service
- Producing a new serious and organised crime strategy.
- Creating street-level crime maps to give the public up-to-date, accurate information on what is happening on their streets so they can challenge the police on performance.

Government measures to prevent crime include those listed below:

- Creating the child sex offender disclosure scheme, which allows anyone concerned about a child to find out if someone in their life has a record of child sexual offences.
- Legislating against hate crime.
- Using football banning orders to stop potential troublemakers from travelling to football matches, both at home and abroad.

Tackling crime in Scotland

Scottish crime figures 2013/14

270,397 recorded crimes – a 40-year low

6785 violent crimes – down 10%

61 murders and culpable homocides

8604 sex crimes – up 12%, with increased reporting

137,324 crimes of dishonesty – housebreaking, shoplifting and theft

Police Scotland

In Scotland it appears that improvements are also evident

As part of 'The Strategy for Justice in Scotland', published in September 2013, the Scottish Government and Police Scotland have introduced or extended a range of policies to reduce crime or improve crime prevention including:

- Policies to tackle antisocial behaviour.
- Policies on counteracting the threat of terrorism.
- New laws to give greater protection to victims of forced marriage.
- Tougher sanctions on crime linked to racial, religious or social prejudice.
- Protecting children from exploitation and dealing with extreme materials.

- Policies on tackling prostitution and kerb-crawling offences.
- Tackling misuse of firearms and air weapons in Scotland.
- Policies to steer young people away from trouble: Kick It Kick Off (KIKO).

The 'Kick It Kick Off' campaign aims to steer young people away from trouble

TOP TIP

For further information on crime levels and measures to tackle crime use the following links:
- www.crimesurvey.co.uk
- www.scotland.gov.uk/Publications/2014/03/9823
- www.gov.uk/government/policies/reducing-and-preventing-crime–2
- www.scotland.gov.uk/Topics/Justice/policies

Quick Test

1. What evidence is there to suggest that crime levels in England and Wales have both decreased as well as increased?

2. What evidence is there to suggest that crime levels in Scotland have both decreased as well as increased?

3. Outline the measures that the UK government has introduced to reduce and prevent crime.

Tackling crime case studies

Tackling hate crime

The UK government reported in 2013–14 that 44,480 hate crimes were recorded by the police, an increase of 5% compared with 2012–2013. They acknowledge that this is not a true picture of the problem as a significant number of hate crimes go unreported.

Hate graffiti

2013–14

The following numbers of hate crimes were reported in 2013–14:

- 37,484 (84%) race hate crimes
- 4622 (10%) sexual orientation hate crimes
- 2273 (5%) religion hate crimes
- 1985 (4%) disability hate crimes
- 555 (1%) transgender hate crimes

(Some of the crimes had more than one motivation, which is why the above numbers total over 100%.)

As a result the UK government have introduced a hate crime action plan named 'Challenge it, Report it, Stop it'. By working with local police, courts, voluntary organisations and an independent advisory group, the UK government aims to meet three objectives:

- Preventing hate crime by challenging the attitudes and behaviours that foster hatred, and encouraging early intervention to reduce the risk of incidents escalating.
- Increasing the reporting of hate crime by building victims' confidence to come forward and seek justice, and working with local and national organisations to make sure the right support is available when they do.
- Working with the agencies that make up the criminal justice system to improve the ways they respond to hate crime.

Reducing knife, gun and gang crime

Gang members carry out half of all shootings in London and are responsible for 22% of all serious acts of violence. The UK government's aim is to reduce gang-related crime and stop young people becoming involved in violence. Measures introduced include:

- New offences of threatening with a knife in a public place or school, which will help improve prosecution rates.

- Dedicated £1.2 million to fund 13 support workers for girls vulnerable to, or suffering from, gang-related sexual violence.

- Gang injunctions for under 18-year-olds made available to the police and local authorities.

- Introduced changes to firearms legislation in the new Anti-social Behaviour, Crime and Policing Bill, which received royal assent in March 2014, creating an offence of possessing illegal firearms for sale or transfer, with a maximum penalty of life imprisonment, and increasing the maximum penalty for manufacture, importation and exportation of illegal firearms.

The 'No Knives, Better Lives' campaign is a Scottish Government initiative that works with local organisations to provide information and support. The campaign aims to raise awareness of the consequences of carrying a knife through interactive means for young people, parents and practitioners. You can find more information on their website: http://noknivesbetterlives.com

TOP TIP

Government strategies to reduce terror-related crimes are covered in Unit 3.

No knives, better lives.
www.noknivesbetterlives.com

The 'No Knives, Better Lives' campaign

Quick Test

1. What evidence is there that the government's measures to tackle hate crime are not effective?

2. Outline the measures taken by the government recently to tackle the issues related to hate crime.

3. What evidence is there that gang crime is a significant problem in cities across the UK?

Alcohol

Alcohol-related crime

Alcohol-related crime and disorder is thought to cost society around £21 billion every year. As a result, the Home Office in July 2013 set out a number of measures to tackle alcohol-related crime and disorder in England and Wales, including minimum pricing and tougher action on irresponsible promotions in pubs and clubs. These were hoped to be introduced by spring 2014. However Crime Prevention Minister Jeremy Browne then indicated that the introduction of a minimum unit price for alcohol will remain a policy under consideration, but will not be taken forward at present and that the UK government will continue to monitor the legal developments around the implementation of the Alcohol (Minimum Pricing) (Scotland) Act 2012. The government has also confirmed it will not be proceeding with a ban on multi-buy promotions in England and Wales (as has been in place in Scotland since 2011) as they believe that evidence does not suggest this would sufficiently curb the most harmful drinking.

Alcohol and crime in Scotland

In 2010, 23% more alcohol was sold per adult in Scotland than in England and Wales, the widest gap to date. The impact of this excessive consumption is estimated to cost Scots £3.6 billion each year; that's equivalent to an incredible £900 for each and every adult in Scotland. The impact on crime and anti-social behaviour is evident, with statistics showing that 45% of prisoners (including 75% of young offenders) were drunk at the time of their offence.

Measures introduced in a bid to control the problem are detailed below.

Alcohol (Minimum Pricing) (Scotland) Act 2012

Passed in June 2012, this Act outlines the plans for the introduction of a preferred minimum price of 50p per unit. This is in relation to crime research from the University of Sheffield that found a proposed minimum price of 50p per unit would result in the following benefits:

- A fall in crime volumes by around 3500 offences per year.
- A financial saving from harm reduction (health, employment, crime etc.) of £942m over 10 years.

Drink driving limit

In 2014 the Scottish Parliament voted unanimously in favour of a law reducing the legal alcohol limit from 80mg to 50mg in every 100ml of blood. The introduction of the new law brought Scotland in line with most other European countries,

The legal alcohol limit has been reduced

however it does make the law different from that in England and Wales. Campaigners for the change suggested that it would cut the number of deaths and serious injuries on the road. The UK government, however, have no plans to reduce the drink drive limit elsewhere in the UK, with the view that it will have no real effect on 'serious offenders'.

Quick Test

1. What is the estimated cost to society of alcohol-related crime and disorder each year?
2. List three reasons that suggest Scotland has a major problem relating to alcohol.
3. Outline how the two measures introduced in Scotland aim to tackle alcohol-related crime.

USA

Background information

Is the USA powerful? Let us look at the facts and figures:

- 9,826,630 square kilometres.
- Approximately half the land area of Russia.
- Slightly larger in area than China.
- UK could fit into the state of Texas alone.
- Population – 317,297,938 (as at January 2014).
- Large variety of water, mineral, agricultural resources.
- Basis for highly productive economy.
- World's wealthiest nation by GDP.
- Leading country in world affairs.
- Influential member of international organisations such as UN and World Bank.
- Leader in number of defence organisations such as NATO.
- Large number of nuclear weapons.
- Perhaps the most powerful military in the world.

The American people

The US population is made up of five main ethnic groups:

- White
- Hispanic
- African American
- Asian and Pacific Islanders (APIs are sometimes discussed as two separate ethnic groups)
- Native American

TOP TIP

Use www.census.gov for quick, easy to access facts about the people, business and geography of the USA.

Quick Test

1. To develop your knowledge of each of the ethnic groups, create a fact file for each group. Include:

   - % of total population
   - Sub groups
   - Settlement patterns
   - Explanation of settlement pattern
   - Key issues facing each group

The political system of the USA

Constitutional arrangements

When the Founding Fathers were writing the constitution they included a whole range of compromises. These ensured that no one person or small group of people would have complete control of government and decision making in the USA. The codified constitution therefore established a full and authoritative set of rules written down in a single text.

What did it establish?

Article I: established **Congress** as the national legislature that would be made up of two chambers, laid down the methods of election, terms of office and powers.

Article II: established a **President** of the USA, laid down methods of election, terms of office and powers.

Article III: established the **US Supreme Court**, laid down the judges' terms of office and their jurisdiction.

Bill of Rights

Attached to the first seven articles were 10 amendments known as the **Bill of Rights**. These were designed to protect American citizens from an over-powerful federal government.

TOP TIP

Use this link to gain further information on the Bill of Rights and what it means for US citizens: http://cdn4.kidsdiscover.com/wp-content/uploads/2012/09/Bill-of-Rights-Kids-Discover.jpg

Separation of powers

The Constitution further guaranteed certain fundamental constitutional rights by separating the power of government into three different 'branches'. The government – federal, state or local – must take steps to ensure that these rights are effectively protected. All three branches of the federal government play an important role.

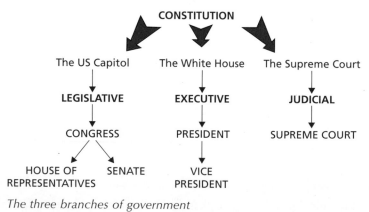

The three branches of government

- Legislative Branch (makes the laws).
- Executive Branch (carries out the laws).
- Judicial Branch (enforces the law and interprets the law).

The Founding Fathers also had the idea that each of these three independent yet equal branches should check the power of the other.

Checks and balances

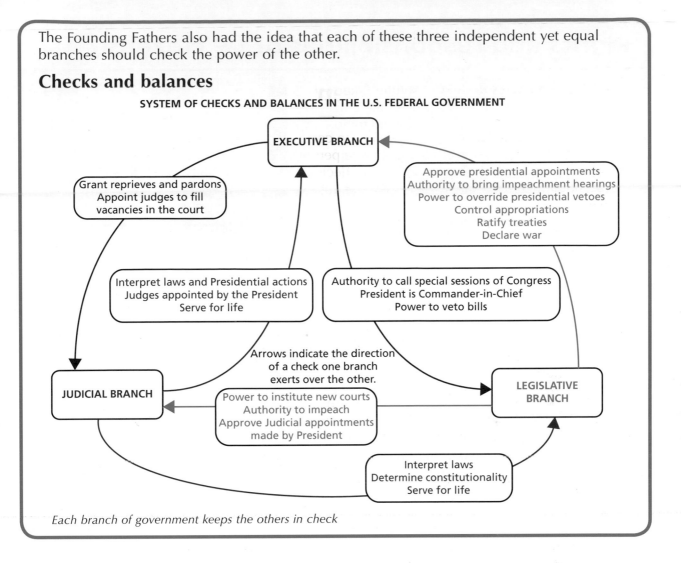

SYSTEM OF CHECKS AND BALANCES IN THE U.S. FEDERAL GOVERNMENT

EXECUTIVE BRANCH

Grant reprieves and pardons
Appoint judges to fill vacancies in the court

Approve presidential appointments
Authority to bring impeachment hearings
Power to override presidential vetoes
Control appropriations
Ratify treaties
Declare war

Interpret laws and Presidential actions
Judges appointed by the President
Serve for life

Authority to call special sessions of Congress
President is Commander-in-Chief
Power to veto bills

Arrows indicate the direction of a check one branch exerts over the other.

JUDICIAL BRANCH

Power to institute new courts
Authority to impeach
Approve Judicial appointments made by President

LEGISLATIVE BRANCH

Interpret laws
Determine constitutionality
Serve for life

Each branch of government keeps the others in check

Rights and responsibilities of US citizens

The first amendments to the Constitution, known as the Bill of Rights, aimed to protect the citizens of the US. The US Citizenship and Immigration Service continues to highlight that all US citizens should be able to exercise and respect certain rights and responsibilities.

Rights

✓ Freedom to express yourself.

✓ Freedom to worship as you wish.

✓ Right to a prompt, fair trial by jury.

✓ Right to vote in elections for public officials.

✓ Right to run for elected office.

✓ Freedom to enjoy 'life, liberty, and the pursuit of happiness'.

Responsibilities

✓ Support and defend the Constitution.

✓ Participate in the democratic process.

✓ Respect and obey federal, state and local laws.

✓ Respect the rights, beliefs, and opinions of others.

✓ Serve on a jury when called upon to do so.

✓ Defend the country if the need should arise.

Every US citizen has certain rights and responsibilities

However due to differing state laws with regard to controversial topics such as gun control, capital punishment and same sex marriage, some US citizens believe their rights are being breached.

Case study: 'Safe Carry Protection Act' – Georgia

In July 2014 Georgia passed a controversial new law allowing weapons in bars, schools, churches and parts of airports. Nicknamed the 'guns everywhere' law it allows teachers to carry guns in the classroom and strengthens the rights of gun owners, forbidding police from stopping people to check their gun permit. Opponents fear that more guns on the street will lead to more victims, not fewer. However the National Rifle Association welcome the support given to gun owners.

Quick Test

1. Using the two diagrams, explain in detail what is meant by the terms 'separation of powers' and 'checks and balances'.

2. Provide evidence (actual examples) of the checks each branch provides on the others.

3. Why do some US citizens believe their rights are being breached?

The powers of the President

The President of the USA

The President of the USA is perhaps the world's best-known public figure and is often referred to as the most powerful person in the world. The powers of the President are set out in Article II of the Constitution and provide him with significant power to govern. However the Constitution, as stated previously, ensures that there are 'checks and balances' on this power.

In 2016 the 45th President will be elected, with some high profile figures declaring that they will be running for office. Former Secretary of State, Hilary Clinton is running for the Democrats and Jeb Bush, former Governor of Florida, along with real estate mogul Donald Trump are both aiming to secure the candidacy for the Republicans.

Barack Obama, 44th President

Head of State

As Head of State the President represents the nation at home and abroad. He has the power and authority to receive other foreign heads of state and offers diplomatic recognition in the exchange of foreign ambassadors. However, these duties as Head of State are more ceremonial and are often not seen as conveying any real or meaningful power.

Patronage

The power of patronage allows the President to appoint secretaries of state to run government departments. In 2013 Obama nominated Chuck Hagel to become the next Secretary of Defence. Presidential power is 'checked' on these occasions by the Senate. The Senate hold nomination hearings and debate the benefits and consequences of such appointments before voting on the final outcome – Hagel's appointment was confirmed 58–41 (1 not voting) in February 2013. The President also has the power to appoint all federal judges.

Legislative function

The President has the power to recommend legislation to Congress – he does this in January of each year at the State of the Union address. President Obama's most high-profile item of legislation has been the Patient Protection and Affordable Care Act – 'ObamaCare'. However Congress can amend, block or even reject items of legislation and the Affordable Care Act is a clear example. President Obama signed the legislation into law in March 2010, however it has been amended significantly since then and has yet to be implemented in full.

Veto

The President has the power to veto bills passed by Congress. He returns the bill to Congress, unsigned, with an explanation of why he has exercised his power. Congress has the choice to either amend the legislation or attempt to overturn the veto. In order to overturn the veto Congress needs to gain a two-thirds majority in both the Senate and the House of Representatives. Since coming to power Obama has only used his veto twice, neither were overridden, while George W. Bush used his power of veto 12 times and was overridden four times.

Executive order

The President can bypass Congress and issue regulations under an executive order. A President would use this in times of emergency or for a particular situation. An executive order has the binding force of the law and requires no congressional approval. Obama has issued a significant number of executive orders since coming to power, including that which ordered the closure of Guantanamo Bay. George W. Bush issued 291 executive orders during his two terms in office, however Congress were able to 'check' this power in terms of investigating his handling of national security issues before and after 9/11.

National security

The President is the Commander-in-Chief of the Armed Forces and is charged with the defence of the USA. He can order the use of troops overseas without declaring war, however he needs congressional approval to officially declare war on a country.

> **TOP TIP**
>
> Use your research skills to gather information on the most recent occasions that the President has exercised his powers and how this power has been checked – it is best practice to have the most up-to-date information.

Quick Test

1. What are the key powers of the US President?
2. How does the President use his position and power to influence the US Congress and the Supreme Court?

Influencing the political system

Opportunities for participation

There are various ways that ordinary Americans can participate in the political system of the USA.

Manning the phones during Obama's campaign

- **Voting** – at federal, state and local levels there are regular opportunities to take part in democratic elections. Approximately 450,000 elections are held in the USA each year. Many elections, such as those for state governor or major city mayors, attract significant media attention. However those for school boards and city councils have a low profile.

- **Standing as a candidate** – US citizens may choose to run as a candidate for a number of positions, including congressman or woman, or state governor.

- **Supporting a candidate** – party members can get involved in the political campaign of a candidate by delivering leaflets, displaying posters or canvassing through a 'phonebank'. Candidates rely on this support for success.

- **Contributing to party funds/campaign** – during the 2012 presidential campaign high profile celebrities as well as ordinary citizens made huge contributions to both Democrats and Republicans. Black Eyed Peas singer will.i.am gave the maximum $61,600 donation to the Democrats and the maximum $5000 to Obama.

- **Joining an interest group** – interest groups attempt to put pressure on the government and influence the amendments or introduction of laws. Interest groups will use methods such as marches, demonstrations and petitions to attract support for their cause. They may also lobby congressmen and women or use the media to publicise their campaign for political change. High profile interest groups in the USA gain huge amounts of publicity and are often perceived to be highly influential. Examples include: The National Rifle Association (NRA), the Coalition to Stop Gun Violence (CSGV) and The American Association of Retired Persons (AARP).

TOP TIP

Ensure that you have a sound knowledge of a current interest group in the USA. The following link will be useful: www.bbc. co.uk/scotland/education/ms/ usa/reference/people/groups. shtml. You should aim to find out who they are, what their main cause for concern is, how they have attempted to gain publicity and whether or not they have been influential.

Fair and equal participation?

Participation in the USA is not always consistent and therefore neither is the political influence of American citizens. Before voting, citizens must register to vote. This appears to be the first issue regarding influence.

In 2012 only 65% of Americans were actually registered to vote, with blacks and Hispanics having lower registration rates than whites. This is often attributed to the fact that the registration procedure can be complicated and some groups don't value voting and so don't see the point in registering. As a result turnout is never as high as it could be. In 2012, of those registered to vote, approximately only 58% actually voted. Some Americans don't vote due to 'voting fatigue' – a high number of official posts are elected and people are put off by elections occurring so often. Certain Americans, such as blacks and Hispanics, do not feel voting will change their lives or improve their situation so they do not value the electoral process. Furthermore many Hispanics are illegal immigrants and are therefore not eligible to vote (the most recent Pew Research suggests that there are approximately 11.1 million illegal immigrants in the USA, over 80% of whom are Hispanic/Latino – approximately 9 million).

Influence of ethnic minorities

In 2008 ethnic minorities increased voter registration and turnout as a result of Barack Obama being the first non-white candidate nominated by either of the two main political parties to run for President. Of the black Americans who voted, 95% voted for Obama along with 66% of Hispanics. It was also evident that Obama was aiming to attract the support of the minority groups with the appointment of a number of ethnic minorities to his first Cabinet including Eric Holder (black), Ken Salazar (Hispanic) and Gary Locke (API). By 2012 the proportion of black people voting for Obama had dropped slightly to 93% with Hispanics increasing to 77%, suggesting that the vote of the minority groups remained significant, given that 59% of white voters voted in favour of Mitt Romney.

Ethnic minorities in 114th Congress

At first glance, the graph implies a certain level of progress for ethnic minorities, with a record number being elected to Congress in 2015. However ethnic minorities actually only make up 17% of Congress (6 Senators (6%) and 85 (20%) members of the House) yet they make up 38% of the total US population.

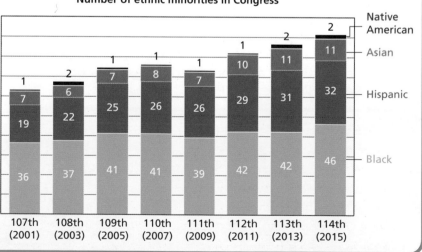

Number of ethnic minorities in Congress

	107th (2001)	108th (2003)	109th (2005)	110th (2007)	111th (2009)	112th (2013)	113th (2013)	114th (2015)
Native American								2
Asian	1	2	1	1	1	1	2	11
Hispanic	7	6	7	8	7	10	11	32
Black	19	22	25	26	26	29	31	46
	36	37	41	41	39	42	42	

How influential are minority groups overall?

It may be that minority groups have more influence than you would first think. In Congress the minority vote can be influential – in the House of Representatives 218 votes are required to pass a bill. Minorities, if they make a united stand, can provide almost 40% of the votes required.

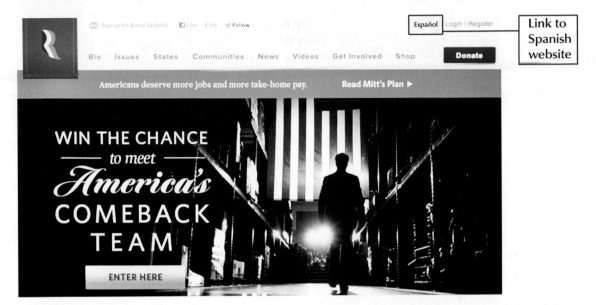

In a bid to attract the Hispanic vote, the Romney campaign launched a Spanish version of their website

Ethnic minorities overwhelmingly vote Democrat as a result of their policies and strategies, which have been devised to support ethnic minorities and the issues they face (poverty, poor healthcare etc.). In turn white candidates/congressmen and women may well support these policies given that they will rely on the votes of minorities in their congressional districts or local areas. Furthermore it is evident that the support is valued, looking at the number of ongoing strategies adopted to encourage ethnic minorities to register and turn out to vote – 'Vote or Die' and 'Declare Yourself' were prominent campaigns in the past and Spanish language campaign materials as well as Spanish language registration forms are used to court the Hispanic vote.

Quick Test

1. Explain why it is reasonable to suggest that American citizens have a number of opportunities to participate in politics.

2. What evidence is there to suggest that Americans do not participate in politics as fully as they could?

3. Outline three pieces of evidence that would suggest ethnic minorities are actually more influential in politics than it would sometimes seem.

Social and economic issues in the USA: health and housing

The idea of the 'American Dream' suggests that there are opportunities for all American citizens to prosper and experience a comfortable, healthy lifestyle. However this is not always the case in reality. Inequality is a continued problem facing the USA and affects citizens in a variety of different ways.

Health and healthcare

Unlike the UK there is no national health service in the USA. American citizens have been, until recently, responsible for meeting the cost of healthcare when they require it. This has led to extensive inequalities in relation to health and access to healthcare.

A significant number of Americans receive health insurance as part of their employment package (44.5% in 2012) however this has decreased in recent years. Others are entitled to government health programmes such as Medicare, Medicaid and State Children's Health Insurance. However this does not account for everyone, with only 25.6% of the population being eligible to access these government programmes in 2012.

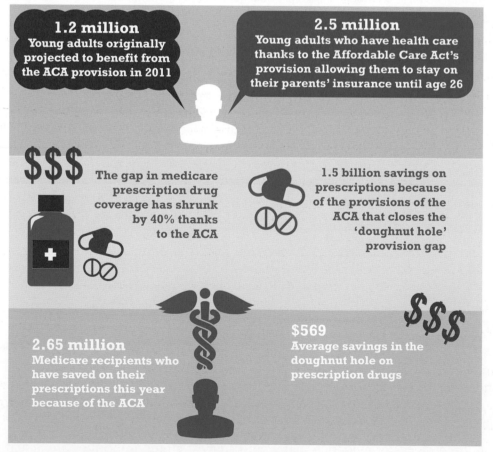

The statistics on 'Obamacare'

Even with the implementation of the Affordable Care Act (known as 'Obamacare', there are still a huge number of uninsured American citizens. In February 2014 the Centers for Disease Control and Prevention (www.cdc.gov) reported that the number of citizens under 65 who were still uninsured stood at 45.2 million (16.9% of the population) with only 61% of the population having private insurance. Ethnic minorities were the least likely to be insured, with almost 30% of Hispanics having no arrangements for cover. Blacks and Asians were also less likely to be insured than whites. This has an impact on children, with approximately 7 million children living without insurance in 2014. The consequences of this continue, with health issues growing throughout life, leading to lower life expectancy.

A recent report in the *New York Times* states that around 10 million more Americans now have health insurance as a result of the Act, with the biggest winners being those aged between 18 and 34, blacks, Hispanics and people who live in rural areas. The areas with the largest increases in coverage include rural Arkansas and Nevada, Southern Texas, large areas of New Mexico, Kentucky and West Virginia and many areas of California and Oregon.

It is hoped that health inequalities will decrease in time as a result of the Act, as currently ethnic minorities suffer poorer health overall and lower life expectancy. Black children for instance have twice the rate of infant mortality of white children.

There is also evidence that ethnic minorities suffer disproportionate rates of health-related issues such as obesity, HIV and AIDS, with black women suffering the highest rates of death from lung cancer, heart disease and strokes.

Housing

Prior to the economic downturn home ownership levels had reached their highest levels in history. Many Americans, including ethnic minorities, were able to afford to live in middle class, relatively crime free suburbs. Many ethnic minorities had integrated into predominantly white neighbourhoods and were experiencing the benefits of suburban living – high quality housing and education with open spaces for children and families to enjoy. On the other hand a significant number of Americans experience substandard housing, especially in the ghettos/barrios, where there are high rates of unemployment, poverty, violence and gang culture; the population of these areas are predominantly ethnic minorities. For example Melrose-Morrisiana, a borough of the Bronx, is the most deprived neighbourhood in New York; here the majority of the population is Hispanic and mainly Puerto Rican and five low-income housing projects exist. In the Bronx overall, where according to the 2010 Census almost 90% of the population are of a minority ethnic group, 100 low-income housing projects exist, encompassing 44,500 apartments.

Homelessness

In the past Americans were often homeless as a result of mental health issues or substance abuse. However the economic crisis of 2008 resulted in thousands of Americans becoming unemployed and losing their homes because they had high risk mortgages that they were no longer able to pay. Due to the lack of affordable housing many Americans became homeless. With the demand for homeless accommodation outweighing the supply a number of Americans resorted to temporary measures of accommodation, often referred to as 'tent cities'.

Temporary accommodation for the homeless

One recent report stated that there were nearly 2.5 million homeless children in the US – that is, one in 30 – and makes a clear reference to the relationship between homelessness and ethnic minorities, and the potential long-term impact. The report states, 'factors that cause the high rates of child homelessness included high rates of family poverty, particularly in houses headed by single women who are black or Hispanic; … and institutional racism resulting in economic segregation'. Children born into these situations will often find it very difficult to break this 'poverty cycle'.

TOP TIP

Read the following news article for further information on homelessness on a state-by-state basis: www.theguardian.com/us-news/2014/nov/17/report-one-in-30-us-children-homeless

Quick Test

1.   Outline how Americans had, until recently, accessed healthcare.
2.   List three pieces of evidence that indicate health inequalities for ethnic minorities.
3.   What has led to the increasing numbers of homeless people in the USA?

Social and economic issues in the USA: education, employment and poverty

Education

Large numbers of Americans view education as the route to achieving the 'American Dream'. Most notably whites and Asians have the highest levels of success in education with blacks and Hispanics less so, creating further long-term inequalities.

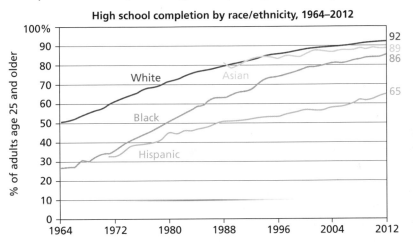

High school completion by race/ethnicity, 1964–2012

Asians are fast becoming the highest achievers with regard to education and outperform whites on many occasions. However even within this ethnic group there are inequalities – South Korean and Japanese young people do better than Cambodians and Vietnamese for example. This is often as a result of stability in the household (higher levels of income on average, and cultures where a strong work ethic and education are valued) in the former groups.

The main reasons for these continuing inequalities are attributed to substandard schools and lack of resources, with the location of the school often being a major factor. Areas of deprivation, as noted above, have higher levels of ethnic minorities and often language barriers exist. Schools in these areas fail to attract and retain high performing students and teachers, ultimately leading to higher drop-out rates and poorer levels of attainment.

Dropout rates

The graph below shows the percentage of 16- to 24-year-olds who are not enrolled in school or have not earned a high school diploma.

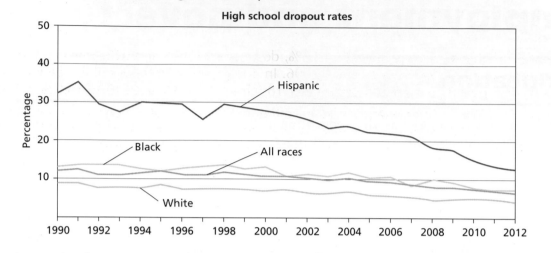

High school dropout rates

In each year the dropout rate was lower for whites than ethnic minorities and although the rates have declined for each group overall there are still huge numbers of ethnic minorities with no formal qualification.

Poverty and unemployment

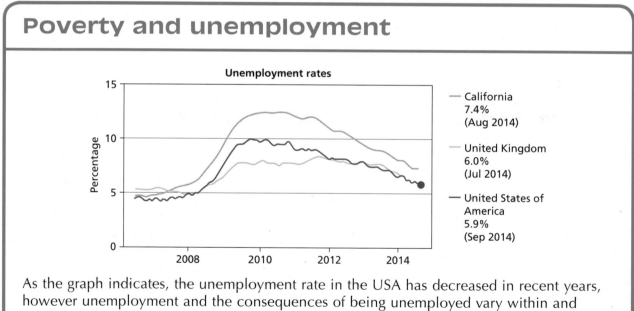

Unemployment rates

California
7.4%
(Aug 2014)

United Kingdom
6.0%
(Jul 2014)

United States of
America
5.9%
(Sep 2014)

As the graph indicates, the unemployment rate in the USA has decreased in recent years, however unemployment and the consequences of being unemployed vary within and between ethnic groups (see next page).

Unemployment rates by ethnic group:

- White: 5.3% (9.0% in 2011)
- Black: 11.7% (16.5% in 2011)
- Hispanic: 7.3% (12.5% in 2011)
- Asian: 4.5% (6.8% in 2011)

In 2013 the official poverty rate was 14.5%, down from 15.0% in 2012. This was the first decrease in the poverty rate since 2006. In 2013 there were 45.3 million people in poverty. The poverty rate for children under 18 fell from 21.8% in 2012 to 19.9% in 2013.

The graph below highlights that blacks have the highest levels of poverty, closely followed by Hispanics, with whites and Asians less likely to live in poverty. As a result blacks and Hispanics are more likely to experience inequality. Why is this the case?

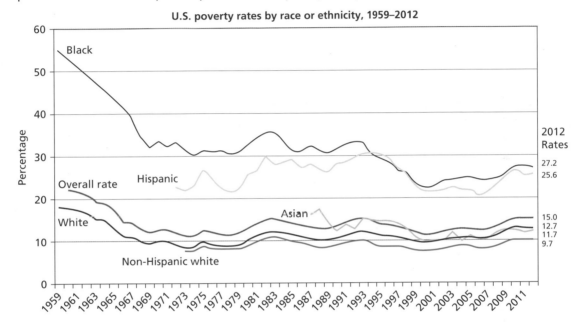

U.S. poverty rates by race or ethnicity, 1959–2012

Black poverty

Black Americans have traditionally been the victims of racism and discrimination and as a result have often found it difficult to progress socially and economically. Many black Americans live in ghettos and this is associated with limited opportunities in education, poorer healthcare and less chance of a fair trial; a disproportionately high level of convicted criminals in America are black with a 2009 study showing that 4.7% of black male adults were in prison compared to 0.7% of white adult males.

Hispanic poverty

Different sub-groups within this ethnicity face different challenges. Mexicans and Puerto Ricans are more likely to live in poverty than Cubans.

Factors leading to poverty

- Unemployment
- Low educational attainment
- Discrimination
- Single parent families
- Welfare cutbacks
- Poverty cycle

Poverty can often be attributed to low income. In 2012 it was clear that blacks and Hispanics earned far less than whites, however the growing income of the Asian population was evident (see figure below).

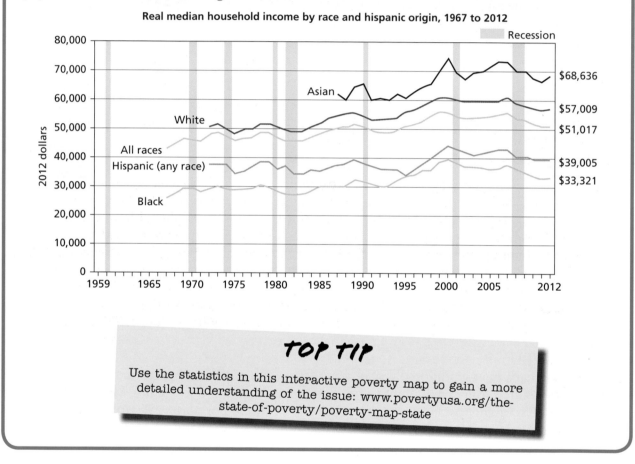

Real median household income by race and hispanic origin, 1967 to 2012

TOP TIP

Use the statistics in this interactive poverty map to gain a more detailed understanding of the issue: www.povertyusa.org/the-state-of-poverty/poverty-map-state

Quick Test

1. Outline the main reasons given for continuing inequalities in relation to education.
2. Using the figure headed 'High School Completion' on page 144 draw a conclusion about the link between ethnicity and educational attainment.
3. Using the figures above, what evidence is there that blacks and Hispanics continue to face higher levels of inequality and poverty?

Social and economic issues in the USA: immigration

Immigration in the USA

Immigration is, and always will be an issue that deeply divides American citizens. In 2013 the US accepted 990,553 people and granted them lawful permanent residence. Approximately 40% of these 'new citizens' were born in Asia. The top countries of origin were:

- Mexico (14%)
- China (7.2%)
- India (6.9%)
- Philippines (5.5%)

Immigration continues to be an issue that deeply divides American citizens

The top US states where legal permanent residents settle are California (19.4%), New York (13.5%), Florida (10.4%), Texas (9.4%) and New Jersey (5.4%). However alongside these legal immigrants there are a significant number of illegal immigrants. In 2012 the Department for Homeland Security estimated that there were 11.4 million unauthorised immigrants living in the USA, with the majority coming from Mexico (59%), El Salvador (6%) and Guatemala (5%). In 2013, 662,483 unauthorised immigrants were apprehended – more than 64% were from Mexico. As a result the US has witnessed a shift in attitude to immigration with recent legislation appearing to signify a more stringent approach. Increases in border security and the introduction of the US Patriot Act have all come out of this shift. Some individual states such as Arizona have also felt it necessary to implement further new legislation. Some of these laws, for example a 2010 law requiring immigrants to carry their papers at all times, have been challenged and deemed unconstitutional by the Supreme Court. Recently President Obama outlined a plan 'to build a fair, effective and common sense immigration system', with four key principles:

1. Continue to strengthen border security.
2. Streamline illegal immigration.
3. Earned citizenship.
4. Crackdown on employers hiring undocumented workers.

Full details of the plan can be found at www.whitehouse.gov/issues/immigration

Obama's plan is to build a fair immigration system

Continued immigration

Arguments for:	Arguments against:
• Contribution to the economy. • Source of cheap labour. • Enterprise culture. • Cultural diversity.	• Burden on the economy. • Poorly paid workers – keep wages low. • Demise of 'American culture'. • Terrorism.

TOP TIP

Ensure that you have a detailed understanding of the arguments for and against immigration and the responses by state and federal governments to immigration – this may be a question in the final Exam.

Quick Test

1. From where do the majority of immigrants to the USA come?
2. How many 'unauthorised' immigrants are estimated to be living in the USA?

Government responses to socio-economic inequalities

American Recovery and Reinvestment Act

In direct response to the economic crisis, Congress passed the American Recovery and Reinvestment Act (often referred to as the 'stimulus' or the 'stimulus package') in February 2009.

The US government stated that the three immediate goals of the Recovery Act were to:

- Create new jobs and save existing ones.
- Spur economic activity and invest in long-term growth.
- Foster unprecedented levels of accountability and transparency in government spending.

The Recovery Act intended to achieve those goals by providing funding for:

- Tax cuts and benefits for millions of working families and businesses.
- Funding for entitlement programmes, such as unemployment benefits.
- Funding for federal contracts, grants and loans.

The *Washington Post* published an article in February 2014 highlighting the relative successes of the Act. The article can be found at: www.washingtonpost.com/blogs/plum-line/wp/2014/02/17/the-stimulus-act-was-a-success-and-we-need-another

Affordable Care Act – 'Obamacare'

In March 2010 President Obama signed the Affordable Care Act. This law put in place comprehensive health insurance reforms, aiming to extend health insurance coverage to some of the estimated 16% of the US population who lack it. The Affordable Care Act is working to make healthcare more affordable, accessible and of a higher quality for families, the elderly, businesses, and taxpayers alike. This includes previously uninsured Americans

Benefits of the Affordable Care Act for Americans

Improving quality and lowering healthcare costs
- Free preventive care
- Rx discounts for seniors
- Protect against healthcare fraud
- Small business tax credits

New consumer protections
- Pre-existing conditions
- Consumer assistance

Access to healthcare
- Health insurance marketplace

Affordable Care Act benefits

and Americans who had insurance that didn't provide them with adequate coverage and security.

This website highlights the key features of the Act year by year: www.hhs.gov/healthcare/facts/timeline/timeline-text.html

The law requires all Americans to have health insurance but offers subsidies to make coverage more affordable and aims to reduce the cost of insurance by bringing younger, healthier people into the health insurance system. Figures released in September 2014 highlighted that 7.3 million people had paid their monthly premium, more than had been anticipated. By September 2015, this had risen to 17.6 million.

Temporary Assistance for Needy Families (TANF)

Designed to help needy families achieve self-sufficiency, this programme sees states being given money from the US government in the form of a block grant. They are then given the task of creating welfare programmes that accomplish at least one of the four purposes of TANF:

- To provide assistance to needy families so that children can be cared for in their own homes.
- To reduce the dependency of needy parents by promoting job preparation, work and marriage.
- To prevent and reduce the incidence of out-of-wedlock pregnancies.
- To encourage the formation and maintenance of two-parent families.

In Washington TANF provides temporary cash and medical help for families in need. Other families participate in the WorkFirst Program, which aims to help families find and keep jobs. The WorkFirst Program assists by helping pay for child care expenses through the Child Care Subsidy Program. It also helps with completing applications and sometimes can provide training to help the unemployed back into work.

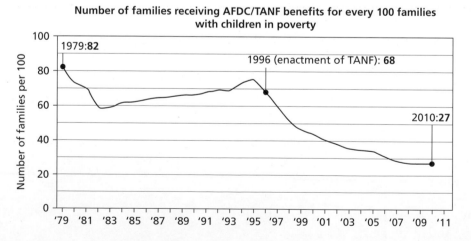

Number of families receiving AFDC/TANF benefits for every 100 families with children in poverty

TANF is based on family size and income. A family of three in Washington with no income would receive a monthly TANF grant of $478. As of August 1997, TANF families are limited to five years of benefits in their lifetime unless they qualify for a time limit extension. The graph (left) highlights the decline in TANF recipients – a direct result of the time limit being introduced.

No Child Left Behind

Passed into law in 2001, NCLB supports 'standards based' education whereby high standards are set and measurable goals put into practice, in order to improve overall performance, offering the promise of better schooling for ethnic minorities and the poor. The Act requires states to develop assessments in basic skills. If assessment scores are continually poor then action is taken to improve schools. Schools may be regarded as 'in need of improvements' and are required by the state to develop a two-year improvement plan in subject areas that are regarded as poor. Should the school fail to meet the set targets for five consecutive years they may be closed down, taken into the care of a private company or the state education department may choose to run the school itself. The law further requires all teachers to be 'highly qualified'. All teachers must be fully qualified in the subject they teach and have evidence to prove this. However 14 years later success is debatable, with critics suggesting the law is too heavily focussed on standardised testing and that states commonly label schools as failures without providing adequate assistance and support to rectify the situation.

'If we want America to lead in the 21st century, nothing is more important than giving everyone the best education possible – from the day they start preschool to the day they start their career.'

President Barack Obama

Race to the Top

This initiative offers incentives for states to embrace educational reform in order to improve teaching and learning, preparing students for college and careers. Race to the Top has dedicated over $4 billion to 19 states that have created clear plans addressing the four key areas of K-12 (that is kindergarten through to 12th grade) education reform, outlined below:

1. Development of rigorous standards and better assessments.
2. Adoption of better data systems to provide schools, teachers, and parents with information about student progress.
3. Support for teachers and school leaders to become more effective.
4. Increased emphasis and resources for the rigorous interventions needed to turn around the lowest-performing schools.

These 19 states serve 22 million students and employ 1.5 million teachers in 42,000 schools, representing 45% of all K-12 students and 42% of all low-income students nationwide.

TOP TIP

Use the link to gain further information on educational initiatives in the USA: www.whitehouse.gov/issues/education/k-12

Food stamps – Supplemental Nutrition Assistance Program (SNAP)

SNAP offers nutritional support to low-income individuals and families as well as their communities. Those eligible receive assistance through an Electronic Benefit Transfer (EBT) card. Benefits are automatically loaded into the household's account each month. People use the SNAP EBT card to buy groceries at authorised food stores. The card works like a bank debit card. The cost of the eligible food items is deducted from the household's account automatically.

The SNAP card is accepted where this sign is displayed

SNAP can be used to buy foods such as bread and cereals, fruit and vegetables, meat, fish and poultry and dairy products. The benefit can also be used to buy seeds and plants that produce food for the household to eat. SNAP cannot however be used to buy any alcohol, cigarettes or tobacco; nor any nonfood items, such as pet foods, soaps, paper products and household supplies.

> ## TOP TIP
>
> You might wish to consider further research into US government departments and their strategies to reduce inequalities, for example the Federal Minimum Wage, the work of the Department of Housing and Urban Development or the Small Business Jobs Act.

Quick Test

1. Why do you think the American Recovery and Reinvestment Act is often referred to as the 'stimulus act'?
2. What are the key purposes of TANF?
3. Outline the key benefits of SNAP.

The role of the USA in international relations

The Role of the USA in the UN, NATO and the G7

The USA is still regarded as the world's dominant military, economic, social and political power. As a result the USA plays a crucial role in each of the international organisations discussed in this chapter.

United Nations

The United Nations websites states: 'The United Nations is an international organization founded in 1945. It is currently made up of 193 Member States … Due to the powers vested in its charter and its unique international character, the United Nations can take action on many of the issues confronting humanity in the 21st century, such as peace and security, climate change, sustainable development, human rights, disarmament, terrorism, humanitarian and health emergencies, gender equality, governance, food production, and more.

An olive wreath surrounds the world in the UN flag

The UN also provides a forum for its members to express their views in the General Assembly, the Security Council, the Economic and Social Council, and other bodies and committees. By enabling dialogue between its members, and by hosting negotiations, the organization has become a mechanism for governments to find areas of agreement and solve problems together.'

Power and influence of USA within the UN
- UN Headquarters is in a US city: New York City.
- The USA is estimated to contribute approximately 22% of the UN's annual budget due to the UN's ability-to-pay scale.
- Permanent member of the Security Council – primary responsibility for the maintenance of international peace and security.
- Under the UN Charter, all member states must comply with Security Council decisions.
- Has the power of veto.

Conflict between US and other member states
Recently it appears that the US has been in conflict with decisions taken and agreements made by the UN. One such example was the US boycott of a UN General Assembly (UNGA) meeting lead by Serbia's former Foreign Minister. While Washington expressed

anger over the debate, 82 other countries took part – making it the most participated-in debate in UNGA history. The US also continually shows opposition to Arab military actions and has shown clear dissent against Security Council resolutions relating to the Israeli–Palestinian conflict.

In 2009 the US government abstained from Security Council Resolution 1860, which called for a halt to Israel's military response to Hamas rocket attacks and the opening of the border crossings into the Gaza Strip.

Conflict also continues with regard to financial arrears – the US in 2014 was estimated to owe the UN peacekeeping budget approximately $337m.

Case study: conflict over Iraq

- Resolution 1441 was made in 2002 regarding the disarmament of Iraq.
- In March 2003 the US, supported by 50 countries, launched military operations against Iraq.
- On 9 April, 2003 Saddam Hussein's regime was overthrown.
- The US argued that this action was authorised by Resolution 1441.
- Other countries maintained that Resolution 1441 did not authorise the use of force without passage of a further resolution.

More recently the Security Council has acted with greater decisiveness. It has imposed sanctions on North Korea and Iran over their nuclear programmes, and authorised a no-fly zone over Libya that helped indirectly to bring down the Gaddafi government.

Cold War fault lines endure, however, as became evident when Russia and China in 2012 vetoed a series of Security Council resolutions aimed at putting pressure on the Syrian regime of President Bashar al-Assad. This has continued to provoke a deep split in the international community, especially with the recent decision taken by the US government to send 300 paratroopers to Ukraine to train 900 national guardsmen. Russian officials have been aggravated by this move and suggest that US presence violates the current ceasefire between Russia and Ukraine.

The future of the US in the UN

US Congress has shown particular concern about reforms related to UN effectiveness and efficiency and in 2010 the US National Security Strategy outlined plans for the future, as detailed below:

'Enhance Cooperation with and Strengthen the United Nations: We are enhancing our coordination with the U.N. and its agencies. We need a U.N. capable of fulfilling its founding purpose – maintaining international peace and security, promoting global cooperation, and advancing human rights. To this end, we are paying our bills. We are intensifying efforts with partners on and outside the U.N. Security Council to ensure timely, robust, and credible Council action to address threats to peace and security. We favor Security Council reform that enhances the U.N.'s overall performance, credibility, and legitimacy.'

NATO

NATO's essential purpose is to safeguard the freedom and security of its members through political and military means. The USA has been a member of NATO since 1949 and it is often referred to as the Atlantic Alliance, creating a situation whereby the security of the US and Europe is linked.

NATO as an organisation is responsible for:

- Decisions and consultations
- Operations and missions
- Partnerships
- Developing the means to respond to threats

The compass rose emblem of NATO

The US has a vital role to play. US troops are deployed in more than 150 countries around the world with approximately 160,000 of its active-duty personnel serving outside the United States and its territories, and an additional 117,000 deployed in various contingency operations.

NATO – Post 9/11

The events of 11 September, 2001 brought about significant change within NATO – member states are now poised to face the challenges of the 21st century. That is, continued terror threats, space and cyber threats, alongside lone-wolf terrorists as well as energy security.

G7

Until 2014 the eight most powerful countries in the world were known as the G8 – Canada, France, Germany, Italy, Japan, Russia, the UK and the USA. It aims to tackle global issues through discussions at the annual G8 summit. In 2014 the G8 summit was suspended as a result of the Crimean crisis and Russia has since been excluded from the G8 countries. The remaining seven countries (the G7) continue to meet annually.

The flags of the original G8 member states

Quick Test

1. List three key features that highlight the power and influence the US has in the UN.
2. Describe how recent issues have caused conflict between the US and other UN member states.
3. Outline how the US intends to work with the UN in the future.
4. Use nato.int/cps/en/natolive/events_77648.htm to assess the work of NATO post 9/11 and the contribution it has made to the 'war on terror'. Make a note of the key events that have taken place. Is the fact that the US is a member of NATO a key factor in this? Explain your answer.

Terrorism

Internationally there is no agreed definition of terrorism, however in the UK the Terrorism Act (2000) defines terrorism as:

'The use or threat of action designed to influence the government or an international governmental organisation or to intimidate the public, or a section of the public; made for the purposes of advancing a political, religious, racial or ideological cause; and it involves or causes:

- Serious violence against a person.
- Serious damage to a property.
- A threat to a person's life.
- A serious risk to the health and safety of the public.
- Serious interference with or disruption to an electronic system.'

In more recent years countries worldwide have witnessed increasing terrorist threats and attacks and terrorism continues to pose a serious and sustained problem for all those involved. As a result of this continued threat the UK government publicises the level of threat they believe we are under, in order for the UK public to remain alert to potential attacks. This publication of information came in the aftermath of the 7 July, 2005 attack on the London transport system.

Threat levels

- **Low** – an attack is unlikely.
- **Moderate** – an attack is possible, but not likely.
- **Substantial** – an attack is a strong possibility.
- **Severe** – an attack is highly likely.
- **Critical** – an attack is expected imminently.

The threat level from international terrorism was raised to severe in the UK in August 2014. This threat level is continually monitored and reviewed by government agencies, based on intelligence gathered and terrorist activities occurring in the international community. Assessments of the international threat level are made by the Joint Terrorism Analysis Centre, while the UK Security Service is responsible for setting the threat levels for Irish and other domestic terrorism. Since September 2010 the threat levels for Northern Ireland-related terrorism have also been made available.

International terrorism

Country threat
- ■ CRITICAL
- ■ SEVERE
- ■ SUBSTANTIAL
- ■ MODERATE
- ■ LOW

The colour-coded threat levels

Quick Test

1. Where does the UK outline its definition of terrorism?
2. List the five main outcomes that could occur as a result of a terrorist attack.
3. Why does the UK government publicise the threat level for international terrorism?

Causes of terrorism

It is evident that the causes of terrorism and terrorist activities are varied, and it is widely recognised that those committing terrorist acts are doing so for a particular cause or purpose, coercing society into change by attracting attention and public acknowledgement of their cause by means of intimidation, threat and violence.

Four key causes

Social and political injustice

Terrorists act on the assumption that they believe they have been stripped of something they are entitled to, such as certain rights or access to land.

Religious beliefs

Religious causes have been the motivation for a number of terrorist attacks. Terrorists in these situations believe they are avenging what they perceive as an attack on their religious beliefs. We have to be mindful of the fact that it is not always one religion attacking another; attacks in Northern Ireland that were linked to the troubles between Protestants and Catholics are a clear example of this, given that both groups would be regarded as Christians.

Ideological beliefs

A number of groups have engaged in terrorism to advance the ideology they believe in, which is not necessarily political or religious, e.g. animal rights campaigners. The Animal Liberation Front (ALF), established in 1976, has taken responsibility for a number of serious attacks, including extreme vandalism and arson and putting innocent peoples' lives at risk. The ALF do this in a bid to meet their aim of inflicting economic damage on those who profit from the misery and exploitation of animals, and in order to liberate animals from places of abuse, i.e. laboratories, factory farms, fur farms etc., and to place them in good homes where they may live out their natural lives, free from suffering. In 2012 an ALF branch in New Zealand took responsibility for a fire that badly damaged a KFC restaurant – this was a response to the purchase of chickens from farms accused of animal cruelty.

ALF logo

Socio-economic factors

Deprivation and related factors such as poverty or a lack of education are now regarded as causes that can drive people to engage in terrorist activities. Researchers suggest that individuals in these situations may be easier to recruit as a result of their socio-economic status.

Quick Test

1. Summarise the four key causes of terrorism.
2. What evidence is there to prove that religious attacks are not always one religion against another?
3. Outline the behaviour displayed by the ALF that would constitute terrorism.

Religious extremism

The 2014 the Global Terrorism Index suggested that during the previous 12 years religious extremism had overtaken national separatism as the main cause for terrorist attacks; 18,000 deaths were recorded in 2013 as a result of religious extremism, a 60% rise from 2012.

Terrorist organisations

The majority of these attacks were attributed to four main terrorist organisations:

- Islamic State (ISIS) in Iraq and Syria
- Boko Haram in Nigeria
- Taliban in Afghanistan
- Al-Qaeda

While reports highlighted that in certain regions such as Europe and North America the main causes of terrorism were political, in Russia they were as a result of nationalist agendas. The majority of deaths (80%) from terrorism occurred in just five countries – Iraq, Afghanistan, Pakistan, Nigeria and Syria, where a clear religious agenda was present.

Prior to 2000 most attacks were caused by national separatist organisations such as the IRA and Chechen rebels. The numbers of these types of terrorist attacks have remained fairly stable while the growth in religious extremism is evident. Reports argue that this growth has occurred as a result of the number of Islamist groups operating and existing in countries such as Iraq, Afghanistan, Pakistan, Nigeria and Syria.

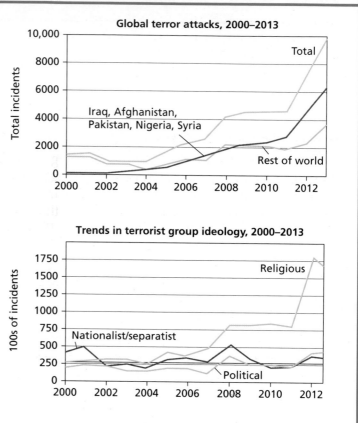

Global terror attacks, 2000–2013

Trends in terrorist group ideology, 2000–2013

Case study: Boko Haram

Boko Haram were established in Nigeria in 2002 and initially focussed their attention on opposing Western education, refusing to send their children to government-run 'Western schools'. As a result they established their own religious complex, comprising of a mosque and Islamic school, enrolling children from local neighbourhoods as well as neighbouring countries. As well as promoting their religious agenda to establish an Islamic state they used this setting as a recruiting ground for jihadis.

Since 2009 Boko Haram have launched a number of attacks on innocent targets, killing more than 5000 civilians. They have been responsible for the abductions of more than 500 men, women and children, including the kidnapping of 276 schoolgirls in April 2014. As a result of their terror approximately 1.5 million people have fled areas where conflict is present. A state of emergency was declared by the Nigerian President in May 2013 in three regions where Boko Haram is strongest – Borno, Yobe and Adamawa, and although an increase in military action was taken their presence and attacks continue to remain strong.

Boko Haram is strongest in Borno, Yobe and Adamawa

It is argued that until the Nigerian government eradicates the high levels of poverty in the country and establishes an education system supported by the people, Boko Haram will continued to exist.

The Global Terrorism Index

The Global Terrorism Index allocates a rating to each country dependent on how affected they are by terrorism. The map below highlights where each country rates in this index, e.g. the UK and USA have higher ratings than other European and North American countries, however they have lower ratings than countries regarded as suffering the highest impact of terrorism such as Nigeria, Pakistan and Afghanistan.

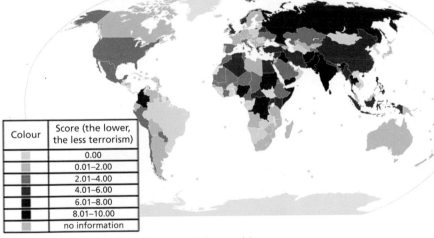

Colour	Score (the lower, the less terrorism)
	0.00
	0.01–2.00
	2.01–4.00
	4.01–6.00
	6.01–8.00
	8.01–10.00
	no information

The Global Terrorism Index's map of the world

TOP TIP

For more information on Boko Haram read the following BBC article: www.bbc.co.uk/news/world-africa-13809501

Quick Test

1. 'Religious extremism was a major cause of deaths in 2013.' What evidence is there to support this view?

2. To which organisations were the majority of religious attacks attributed?

3. Using the two graphs on the previous page draw conclusions about:
   - Global terror attacks within certain countries in comparison to the rest of the world.
   - Trends in ideology-related incidents.

Issues for the future

Although there is evidence that organised religious extremism is on the increase we must not lose sight of other influences that pose a threat.

The 'lone wolf'

This is someone who commits or is suspected of committing an act of terror in support of a recognised terrorist organisation or movement. The difference is that they normally do so without any financial or material help from such groups. It is often argued that a lone wolf represents a greater threat to countries than organised movements, given that individuals could go undetected as they actually may never come into contact with the group they support.

The Boston marathon attack

- Anders Breivik killed 77 people in Norway in 2011. Impersonating a police officer, he shot and killed 69 people attending the summer camp of the youth organisation of the Labour Party, having earlier killed eight people with a car bomb placed in the Norwegian government headquarters in Oslo.

- Dzhokar and Tamerlan Tsarnaev set off two pressure cooker bombs at the finish line of the Boston marathon in April 2013, in an act to avenge the wars in Iraq and Afghanistan, killing three people and wounding over 260 others.

Terrorist cells

A cell is a very small group of terrorists operating together in a specific area. They are often referred to as the 'building blocks' for a larger network or terrorist organisation. The cell may be linked only to a group leader and may be completely unaware of other cells operating close by. Five Belgian nationals were arrested in 2015 for participation in a terrorist organisation linked to ISIS. It is believed the small group were on the brink of an attack.

Home-grown terrorism

Home-grown terrorism or domestic terrorism is associated with acts of violence committed by citizens of the same country they attack. In a bid to instill terror in the people and government of France, brothers Said and Cherif Kouachi attacked the staff of the Charlie Hebdo magazine in Paris in January 2015, killing 11 people and injuring 11 others. Shortly afterwards they killed a policeman. The attacks were in response to the publication of satirical cartons of the prophet Muhammad.

The Charlie Hebdo building in Paris was attacked in January 2015

Quick Test

1. Why is a lone wolf regarded as a significant threat to security?
2. Why are terrorist cells referred to as 'building blocks'?
3. What was the motivation for the attack on the Charlie Hebdo magazine staff in Paris?

Consequences of terrorist activities: individuals

> *'Terrorism is a worldwide problem. It is not just confined to the UK or Europe. It is motivated by a wide variety of causes, not just one particular religious, nationalist or ideological cause.'*
>
> **The UK Security Service**

Individuals

Terrorism at its most extreme can cause loss of a loved one or an entire family, and the threat of continued terrorist attacks induces fear in individuals worldwide. This fear can often result in irrational behaviour, such as fear of flying or the potential to feel under threat for your safety. In addition individuals can develop a hatred of certain groups or individuals, for example 'Islamophobia', threatening the rights afforded to individuals. A report commissioned by the Equality and Human Rights Commission in 2011 found that Muslims felt that as a result of UK government counter-terror measures they were being treated as a 'suspect community', with stereotypical ideas of terrorists continuing to grow.

Research indicates that a certain number of individuals are at risk of radicalisation. A recent study by the University of London found that young Muslim men and women born in the UK who were suffering depression and feeling socially isolated were most vulnerable to recruitment by terrorist organisations; women are just as vulnerable as men. It reported that as many as 60 British females had travelled to Syria to join the group Islamic State (ISIS).

Case study: Aqsa Mahmood

Privately educated, Aqsa Mahmood left her Glasgow home in November 2013 to join ISIS in Syria, where she married an Islamic State (ISIS) fighter. She told her parents she wanted to become a martyr and would see them again on the 'day of judgment'.

Children

Those children who are directly and indirectly involved in terrorism can be particularly vulnerable. Children living in areas where terrorist activities are frequent are at risk of suffering a number of damaging and life-changing experiences, from injury through to losing parents or even death. Furthermore the American Psychological Association (APA) argue that children are at risk of experiencing mental health difficulties after an act of terrorism. This can be true of children who are near to or witness the event or even those who live in the affected area or who have witnessed the event on television. The APA state that children can suffer post-traumatic stress disorder (PTSD), which usually occurs within three months of the event, however can last up to 15 years after the terrorist attack.

A recent study found that six months after 9/11, approximately 75,000 New York City public school children in grades 4–12 were suffering from PTSD, including children who were not directly affected by the event.

Children of Gaza

A recent UN document reported that the month-long offensive in 2014 of Israel against Hamas has had a 'catastrophic and tragic impact' on the children of Gaza. Israel destroyed 142 schools in the short time and killed between 373 and 408 children.
In support of the evidence presented by the APA, UNICEF suggested that those children who survived the conflict will be faced with severe psychological difficulties.

Palestinian children salvage items from the rubble of destroyed buildings in part of Gaza City's al-Tufah neighbourhood

TOP TIP

Follow the link below to read an article on the recent BBC documentary that highlighted the plight of the Children of Gaza:
http://www.telegraph.co.uk/culture/tvandradio/tv-and-radio-reviews/11727208/Children-of-the-Gaza-War-BBC-Two-review.html
Your teacher may have a copy of this documentary that you can borrow.

Quick Test

1. List three ways that terrorism can affect individuals.
2. Outline the problems faced by children as a result of terrorism. Give evidence to support your answer.

Consequences of terrorist activities: countries and their governments

Economic consequences

Terrorism is not confined to one specific country or region, countries worldwide suffer the impact and consequences of terrorism. The Global Terrorism Index (GTI) states that the 'economic costs of terrorism go further than the destruction of property and the loss of life. The increased costs of security, military expenditure and insurance often outweigh the original attack'. These can be categorised into **primary (direct)** and **secondary (indirect)** costs.

Primary (direct) costs:	Secondary (indirect) costs:
• Immediate damage caused. • Loss of life, injury. • Damage to infrastructure.	• Disruptions to economy due to event/threat. • Increased security costs. • Decrease in foreign investment. • Decreased trade. • Decreased tourism.

The effects and costs of 9/11 have been debated widely, however the GTI estimated that the large loss of life and destruction of infrastructure from the attacks totalled $55 billion in New York alone, while secondary effects such as increased security ($589 billion), decreased economic activity ($123 billion) and other costs have been totalled to be as much as $3.3 trillion.

Increased costs of insurance

After 9/11, insurance premiums on large infrastructure within the US increased dramatically. For example, Chicago O'Hare airport's annual insurance policy increased from $125,000 to $6.9 million. Similar costs have been seen in Australia following the Bali bombings, and in the UK, Germany and France.

Increased government spending

Governments often have to take on the financial burden of any terrorist acts that result in damage to property or people. As a result less is spent on other infrastructure investments, and funding given to education and healthcare may be reduced.

Social consequences

Countries, as well as individuals, may suffer the social consequences of terrorism in relation to an increase in fear, homelessness and poverty. Yemen, ranked 8th in the Global Terrorism Index list of countries worst affected by terrorism, is a clear example of the link between terrorism and poverty. The World Bank highlighted Yemen as one of the poorest countries in the Arab world, with the poverty rate increasing from 42% in 2009 to 54.5% in 2012 and being one of the most food-insecure countries globally, with the UN World Food Programme highlighting that 4.5 million Yemenis have a severe lack of access to food and 6 million more have a moderate lack of access. The youth unemployment rate is also around 40%, which links back to the fact that young men and women are vulnerable targets for religious extremists. This could suggest that terrorism contributes to a cyclical pattern of poverty – those in poverty resort to terrorist measures as a response to the poverty they live in, in turn causing further devastation and destruction.

The World Bank highlighted Yemen as one of the poorest countries in the Arab world

Countries such as Japan however have been virtually free from international terrorism, only suffering a small number of attacks, mainly as a result of home-grown terrorists acting against the government. Most notable of these was the 1995 chemical attack on the Tokyo subway system by terrorist organisation Aum Shinrikyo, killing 12 and resulting in thousands suffering after-effects. Two days after the Tokyo subway attack more than 1000 Japanese police stormed the Aum headquarters, discovering a huge stockpile of deadly chemical and biological warfare agents, including enough sarin ingredients to kill 4 million people. Twelve of the leading terrorists were captured, tried and sentenced to death.

However Japan has become the latest country to suffer at the hands of ISIS. A video released in January 2014 appeared to show the killing of one of two Japanese journalists being held hostage by ISIS. The terrorist organisation had demanded a $200m (£133m) ransom for the two hostages.

In 2014 ISIS released videos showing the murder of British hostages David Haines and Alan Hemming, as well as US citizens James Foley, Steven Sotloff and Abdul-Rahman Kassig.

Case study: Islamic State (ISIS)

Supporters of ISIS

ISIS is a Jihadist militant group based in Iraq and Syria. It aims to establish a 'caliphate', or Islamic state in Sunni majority regions of Iraq and Syria. ISIS have seized areas across northern Iraq as a result of large-scale military attacks. The exact size of the group is unclear, however it is thought to have thousands of fighters, with a growing number of individuals worldwide becoming radicalised to their vision. Without stability in Iraq it is feared that ISIS may become a lasting threat, causing regional divides between the Shia, Sunni and Kurdish sections, with potential to create a situation similar to that of Syria.

Paris attacks, November 2015

Isis carried out a series of coordinated attacks across the city, the most deadly terrorist attack in Europe since the Madrid train bombings of 2004. Over 350 people were injured and, at time of writing, 130 people had died. As a result, France declared a state of emergency and retaliated by mobilising 115 000 security personnel, as well as carrying out air strikes on the Islamic State in Syria.

Quick Test

1. Outline the difference between primary and secondary costs of terrorism.
2. Give three pieces of evidence to show primary and secondary costs to the US after 9/11.
3. What are the three main social consequences of terrorism?
4. What evidence is there to suggest a link between poverty and terrorist activities?
5. Outline the recent incidents that have taken terrorism to Japan.

International community

In recent years the international community has had to respond to a number of terrorist attacks, impacting on a number of countries, both directly and indirectly. As a result there is agreement that international terrorism and the threat of further attacks have huge consequences for the international community.

case study: Arab Spring

In December 2010 Mohamed Bouazizi, a young Tunisian man, was stopped by police from selling fruit in the street. He set himself on fire in protest. A few weeks later he died, however his actions encouraged an uprising that saw the downfall of President Ben Ali and paved the way for a number of uprisings and revolutions across the Middle East.

In Egypt, after 18 days of mass protest, President Mubarak was forced to resign after 29 years in power. Anti-government demonstrations in Libya started what was to be the downfall and ultimate death of Colonel Gaddafi after 42 years in power. Although not a terrorist threat in essence it had a major impact on the international community, with the UN Security Council authorising 'all necessary measures' to protect civilians. NATO launched military attacks as well as imposing a no-fly zone.

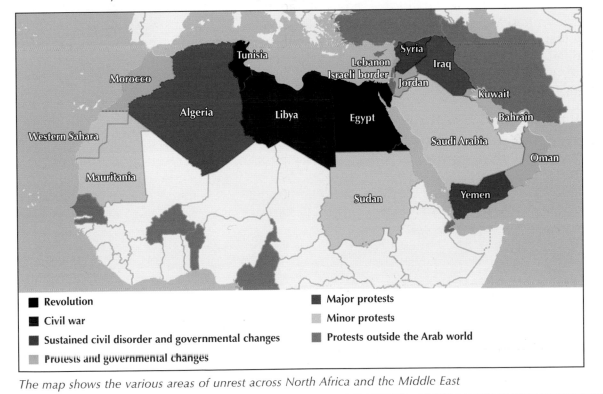

■ Revolution	■ Major protests
■ Civil war	■ Minor protests
■ Sustained civil disorder and governmental changes	■ Protests outside the Arab world
■ Protests and governmental changes	

The map shows the various areas of unrest across North Africa and the Middle East

Similar clashes have been witnessed in Yemen and Syria and continuing issues in these countries suggest the international community will witness long-term violence with a potential threat of increased terrorist attacks. The presence of Al-Qaeda in the Arabian Peninsula (AQAP) caused both the UK and the US to withdraw diplomatic staff from the region in 2013. Furthermore in Syria, the troubles have allowed for an increase in Sunni jihadists as well as the rise of ISIS, with the extremist group taking control of large areas. As a result, a US-led coalition launched air strikes in September 2014.

Quick Test

1. Outline the events of the uprisings in the Middle East, also referred to as the Arab Spring.

2. Use the following link to read a full account of the conflict in Syria and the impact it has had on the international community and terrorism: www.bbc.co.uk/news/world-middle-east-26116868

Resolving terrorism: national attempts

Counter-terrorism in the UK

Throughout 2015 the UK government stated that the risk of a terrorist attack was **severe** – meaning a terrorist attack is highly likely. It is the responsibility of the UK government to protect UK citizens, with the Home Office being the department challenged with this difficult task. A range of measures are in place in an attempt to counter the threat of terrorism.

Home Secretary, Theresa May

CONTEST

The Office for Security and Counter-Terrorism works to counter the threat from terrorism by carrying out the government's counter-terrorism strategy, 'CONTEST'.

The strategy is based on four areas of work:

- Pursue – to stop terrorist attacks.
- Prevent – to stop people becoming terrorists or supporting terrorism.
- Protect – to strengthen our protection against a terrorist attack.
- Prepare – to mitigate the impact of a terrorist attack.

The Home Office report that they are:

- Carrying out a communications capabilities development programme, which will give them the ability to continue to protect the public in the future, as internet-based communications become increasingly widespread.
- Using science and technology to counter the threat from terrorism.
- Supporting the UK security industry to export their products and expertise to other countries hosting major international events.
- Working with the Northern Ireland Office and the relevant authorities in Northern Ireland to help counter the severe threat from terrorism in Northern Ireland.

167

Legislation

The UK government has also passed a number of pieces of legislation in a bid to counter terrorism.

Prevention of Terrorism Act (2005)

This Act established the 'control order' – a form of house arrest.

Terrorism Act (2006)

- Drawn up in the wake of the 7 July bomb attacks in London.
- Attempt to disrupt the training and recruitment of potential terrorists.
- Tony Blair suffered his first Commons defeat as PM when attempting to extend the time police could detain terror suspects without charge to 90 days – parliament agreed in the end to increase the time from 14 days to 28.

The Counter-Terrorism Act (2008)

- Enables police to take fingerprints and DNA samples from individuals subject to control orders.
- Enables police to enter – by force if necessary – and search the premises of individuals subject to control orders.
- Enables the Treasury to direct the financial sector to take action on suspected money laundering or terrorist financing.

Terrorism Prevention and Investigation Measures Act (2011)

- Abolished control orders.
- Introduced 'Terrorism Prevention and Investigation Measures' (TPIMs) – similar to control orders and include the following measures:
  - Electronic tagging, reporting regularly to the police.
  - Living at home, unable to leave overnight.
- TPIMs expire after a maximum of two years unless new evidence emerges of involvement in terrorism.

The Counter-Terrorism Act (2008) enabled police to take fingerprints from people under control orders

Protection of Freedoms Act (2012)

- Repealed the stop and search powers and replaced them with fairer and more specific powers, enabling the police to protect the public but also make sure that there are strong safeguards to prevent a return to the previous excessive use of stop and search without suspicion.
- Reduced the maximum period that a terrorist suspect could be detained before they are charged or released from 28 to 14 days.

Recent measures

In response to the continued and ever-growing threat of terrorism and the unlawful killings of UK citizens by ISIS, Prime Minister David Cameron announced that the UK needed a 'forensic focus' to prevent potential terrorists travelling from the UK as well as returning from conflict zones. He outlined this in response to the fact that an estimated 700 British nationals had travelled to Iraq and Syria to fight alongside Islamic State as well as other militant groups.

Measures announced included:

- Powers to be given to police to confiscate the passports of suspected terrorists at UK borders.
- Introduction of de-radicalisation programmes.
- Blocks in place to prevent suspected British terrorists returning to the UK.
- Airlines would be forced to disclose information about passengers travelling to and from conflict zones.

Quick Test

1. Outline the four areas of work upon which the CONTEST strategy is based.
2. Summarise the main points from the legislation introduced by the UK government in an attempt to combat terrorism.

Resolving terrorism: international attempts

USA

Immediately after 9/11 Congress passed a significant number of laws to support Bush's 'war on terror', outlined below.

- Authorisation for Use of Military Force (2001) – grants the President the authority to use all 'necessary and appropriate force' against those whom he determines 'planned, authorized, committed or aided' the September 11th attacks, or who harboured those persons or groups.

- USA Patriot Act (2001) – broadened the discretion of law enforcement and immigration agencies to detain and deport suspected terrorists, while reducing existing restrictions related to intelligence gathering.

- Creation of Department of Homeland Security (2002) – responsibility for preventing terrorist attacks on the US.

- Military Commission Act (2007) – authorised trial by military commission for violations of the law of war, and for other purposes.

Obama has promised to close Guantanamo Bay before he concludes his second term in office

Further acts were introduced in relation to terror suspects, limitations on the detention of prisoners, definitions of torture and war crimes and during the Bush regime the US came under intense scrutiny around the treatment of detainees at Guantanamo Bay. When Obama came to power in 2009 he issued an executive order promising to close the controversial prison within a year. More than six years later he has reissued that promise with the goal of having it closed before he concludes his term in office. However, he has faced challenges at every turn from Congress in relation to the transfer and release of prisoners, with the House of Representatives voting in 2013, 249–174 to defeat an amendment calling for its shutdown by the end of 2014.

Bureau of Counterterrorism (CT)

The US does however continue to fight the threat of terror with a National Strategy for Counterterrorism, part of the US Strategy for National Security, and also makes international attempts to resolve the issue through the Bureau of Counterterrorism, which aims to forge partnerships with different organisations and foreign governments to develop coordinated strategies to defeat terrorists and secure the cooperation of international partners.

Bureau of Counterterrorism: programmes and initiatives
- Anti-Terrorism Assistance Program (ATA)
- Countering Violent Extremism (CVE)
- Counterterrorism Finance (CTF)
- Foreign Emergency Support Team (FEST)
- Global Counterterrorism Forum (GCTF)
- International Security Events Group (ISEG)

Quick Test

1. What evidence is there to argue that Bush wanted to make an immediate impact in relation to the 'war on terror'?

2. What evidence is there that Obama has failed to deliver on his promises relating to the closure of Guantanamo Bay?

The UN and NATO's responses to terrorism

UN Global Counter-Terrorism Strategy

At the 2005 World Summit, then UN Secretary-General Kofi Annan announced proposals for a comprehensive and effective approach to terrorism. Member states agreed, for the first time, on a clear and unqualified condemnation of terrorism and since then have continued to reiterate the need to uphold and promote the UN Global Counter-Terrorism Strategy, which encompasses four main elements:

- Tackling the conditions conducive to the spread of terrorism.
- Preventing and combating terrorism.
- Building states' capacity to prevent and combat terrorism.
- Ensuring respect for human rights and the rule of law as the fundamental basis of the fight against terrorism.

UN member states take a vote

As the main body safeguarding international law, the UN can play an important role in strengthening legal approaches to terrorism, with the UN Security Council in recent years strengthening the work of its counter-terrorism bodies. Furthermore the UN has adopted a number of resolutions condemning acts of terrorism and terror-related acts, such as Resolution 2170 (2014), which condemns gross, widespread abuse of human rights by extremist groups in Iraq and Syria. On this occasion the UN called for all member states 'to act to supress the flow of foreign fighters, financing and other support to Islamist extremist groups in Iraq and Syria'.

TOP TIP

For further information on the UN Global Counter-Terrorism Strategy follow the link below:
www.un.org/en/terrorism/strategy-counter-terrorism

NATO

NATO recognises terrorism as a 'global threat that knows no border, nationality or religion – a challenge that the international community must tackle together'. NATO has been involved in numerous initiatives and programmes to counter terrorism and works to develop adequate capabilities for its countries in the fight against terror.

NATO (OTAN in French)

Highlights

- NATO invoked its self-defence Article 5 for the first time in response to the terrorist attacks of 9/11 on the United States.
- NATO's immediate response operation, Active Endeavour, was established to deter, detect and, if necessary, disrupt the threat of terrorism in the Mediterranean Sea.
- NATO can provide assistance in securing major public events that might attract the interest of terrorists.
- NATO develops new capabilities and technologies to tackle the terrorist threat and to manage the consequences of a terrorist attack.

TOP TIP

The NATO website has more detailed information on how the organisation is attempting to combat terrorism: www.nato.int/cps/en/natohq/topics_77646.htm

Quick Test

1. What are the four key elements of the UN Global Counter-Terrorism Strategy?
2. What allows the UN to play an important role in strengthening legal approaches to terrorism?
3. Outline the key aims of Resolution 2170.

Effectiveness of measures to combat terrorism

Given the fact that terrorism and terrorist attacks occur on an international scale we have to question how effective measures taken to combat terrorism actually are. We could argue that we have not witnessed anything on the scale of 9/11 again and therefore measures must be working, however the constant threat and occurrence of radicalised groups and individuals would suggest that more should be done.

Case study: terror suspects travel to and return from Syria

Scotland Yard recently released information that suggests up to 700 Britons have travelled to Syria in order to join ISIS, with approximately half having returned to the UK with the threat of causing more violence and fear. Scotland Yard have acknowledged that as of May 2015 the UK is facing the biggest threat from terrorism since the aftermath of 9/11 and as a direct result the number of terrorist-related incidents and terrorism-related arrests have increased. In the UK between April 2014 and March 2015 the number of terror suspects arrested rose by 33% to 338. Scotland Yard acknowledge this level of threat to be complex given that it ranges from the lone wolf suspect to sophisticated networks with coordinated plots, and the fact that not only men but growing numbers of women and children are being drawn to extremism.

Case study: radicalisation

Growing evidence has emerged that radicalisation of many young, potentially vulnerable, male and female citizens is becoming more commonplace. In February 2015 three schoolgirls from Bethnal Green Academy, London, went missing and were later found to have travelled to Turkey and then crossed the border into Syria. Police officers had spoken to the three girls in December 2014, after their 15-year-old friend had run away to a region of Syria controlled by ISIS, and also again in February prior to their disappearance. Their parents later criticised the police for not passing on vital information, however the girls had not been seen as a flight risk.

It is estimated that around 4000 Westerners have joined ISIS, with almost 550 of these being women. Recent research highlighted that ISIS' success at recruiting females should not be disregarded. Through the use of social media, other recruits and extremist theology, young girls are targeted, with the intention of recruiting them into the regime. The ISIS media outlet, Al-Zawra, has been criticised for romanticising the notion of a jihadi fighter seeking the ultimate goal of martyrdom, and by association the wife of a martyr being the closest thing to being a martyr. It is also argued that not only have they been radicalised, they have also ultimately been groomed, with Twitter account Jihad Matchmaker promising to 'link up those seeking marriage in Syria'.

Case study: terrorist plots uncovered

The media have frequently reported a number of terrorist plots being uncovered. In December 2014 it emerged that a 9/11-style attack had been planned for the UK, with Al-Qaeda planning to attack five passenger planes during the Christmas period. The threat was apparently taken so seriously it almost led to an outright ban on all hand luggage and as a country we witnessed a range of measures being put in place such as mobile phones, iPads and tablets having to remain switched on to pass through security.

However a 2015 article in *Time* magazine criticised the US in its fight against terror, suggesting that the US approach was failing badly, with tactics producing more dangerous and more committed extremists. It argued that methods used by the US such as targeted drone strikes, US special forces raids and training small, elite units of local forces were not enough to combat current threats. The article highlighted the fact that extremists today seek revenge for those who have been killed by US forces and to end US support for those they deem to be abusive, corrupt leaders, exemplified by the 'Charlie Hebdo attack, the growing Islamic State, the rampaging Boko Haram, the fractured, chaotic Yemen and the Taliban who massacre schoolchildren'.

TOP TIP

Mapping terrorism: the following link will give you further information about terrorism worldwide: www.mi5.gov.uk/home/about-us/what-we-do/the-threats/terrorism/international-terrorism.html

Quick Test

1. Summarise the key points relating to terrorists travelling to and returning from Syria. What problem does this pose to the UK once they have returned?

2. What methods do terrorist organisations use to entice new recruits?

3. In what ways did the UK government increase airport security in December 2014?

4. Is it possible to suggest that measures to combat terrorism are effective? Explain your answer.